BASEBALL

FIELD GUIDE

An in-depth illustrated guide to the

complete rules of baseball

Dan Formosa & Paul Hamburger

BASEBALL FIELD GUIDE
AN IN-DEPTH ILLUSTRATED GUIDE TO THE COMPLETE RULES OF BASEBALL

Published by
Thunder's Mouth Press
An Imprint of Avalon Publishing Group Inc.
245 West 17th St., 11th Floor
New York, NY 10011

AVALON
publishing group incorporated

Library of Congress Cataloging-in-Publication Data is available.

ISBN: 1-56025-700-8
ISBN 13: 978-1-56025-700-4

9 8 7 6 5 4 3 2 1

Book design by Dan Formosa and Paul Hamburger
Printed in China
Distributed by Publishers Group West

BASEBALL

FIELD GUIDE

An in-depth illustrated guide to the

complete rules of baseball

Baseball Field Guide: Table of Contents

Introduction: How to Use This Book

Overview: The *Baseball Field Guide* is designed and written to be a quick and easy-to-use reference guide to the complete rules of Major League Baseball. It organizes and explains the vague, misleading, confusing, inconsistent, and obscure rules of America's favorite pastime.

The rules of Major League Baseball have evolved over many decades, growing in number and complexity. The official rule book is written to cover every angle and circumstance — but it is not designed to be easily read. The *Baseball Field Guide* is a companion guide, explaining the basic rules, untangling complex rules, and reiterating them in a form that is accessible and useful for any fan, from beginner to expert.

This book is intended to be used as a reference guide.

The information in this book is written and organized to be easily retrieved. Rules are intuitively arranged according to topic and subject.

Each chapter covers a major topic and begins with a list of the contents to be found in that chapter. Important rules are cross-referenced throughout the book. Since many of the more fundamental rules apply to several topics, the same rule may be explained in more than one chapter. In cases where rules are repeated, our explanation discusses the rules from a point of view relevant to that chapter.

This book was not intended to be read from cover to cover — at least not in one sitting. Instead it is designed to allow you to get quick and clear answers to one or two issues at a time. It's a handy book to have around while watching a game — to answer a question, settle an argument, or perhaps win a bet about the true nature of the infield fly rule.

In the long run, we hope this book helps you enjoy the beautiful game of baseball.

Special thanks:

This book was created with the help of many nice people and organizations, including:

Laura Gross, Peter Zubiaurre, Greg Littleton, Lou Fratello, Kimberly Fratello, James Bintliff, Stephen Brandt, Smart Design, and John Oakes.

www.baseballfieldguide.com

1 | Basic Rules of Baseball

This chapter provides preliminary insight into the rules of the game. The first two pages show the basic rules at a glance. Subsequent pages go a bit further — but not much, since this chapter is meant to be a quick guide.

Chapters later in this book discuss the rules of baseball in detail. This chapter is intended to get new fans started.

Basic Rules of Baseball: contents

Baseball At a Glance

Overview: This section provides a quick description of baseball, and shows the basic components of the game, including the field, the players and the equipment. Later in the chapter you can learn more about how the game is played.

Baseball, a quick description

Baseball is played by two teams of nine players each. The objective of the game is to score more runs than the opposing team. A baseball field is arranged with four bases. In counterclockwise order, they are first base, second base, third base, and home plate. A run is scored when a runner touches all bases, reaching home plate.

A baseball game lasts nine innings (additional innings will be played if the score is tied). In each inning both teams will have a chance to bat.

To start the inning, nine fielders will take their positions. The pitcher will throw the ball to a batter from the opposing team, who will try to hit it. The batter will get a strike if he swings and misses, or fails to

swing at a perfectly good pitch. If he gets three strikes, he is out. He will also be out if he hits the ball but his hit is caught by a fielder before it touches the ground. If his hit touches the ground first, however, the batter begins his run around the bases. If other runners are on base they may run as well.

The fielders will attempt to put out the batter or runners as they advance. A runner touching a base, however, is safe on that base and cannot be put out. A team is allowed three outs before the next team will come to bat.

The winning team will be the team with the most runs scored at the end of the game.

The field and players:

The infield

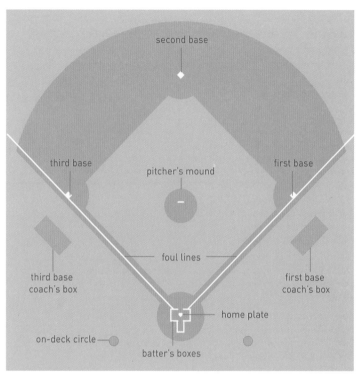

second base

third base

pitcher's mound

first base

foul lines

third base
coach's box

first base
coach's box

home plate

on-deck circle

batter's boxes

Basic equipment

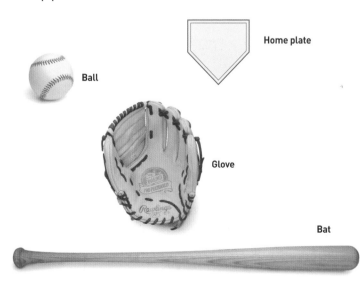

Home plate

Ball

Glove

Bat

Baseball: Basic Rules

Overview: The goal of the team at bat is to reach the next base — hence the name "baseball." If a runner safely reaches first, second, third, and home plate he will score a run for his team.

How to score: The first thing a batter wants to do is to get on a base safely. There are many ways to get on base, but the most typical way is to hit the ball so that none of the fielders can catch it. If the batter does that, he can try to run to a base before a fielder tags him with the ball. If he can continue to advance to all the bases until he makes it back to home plate (where he started), he will score a point for his team.

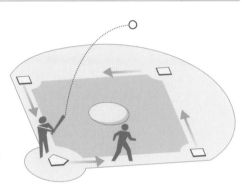

Pitching

The pitcher's job is to throw the ball to the batter, in an attempt to put him out. The pitcher may throw the ball into the strike zone, or may try to throw the ball just outside of the strike zone in hopes the batter will swing but miss. Each pitch thrown by the pitcher will result in either:

• a strike
• a ball
• a hit
• an awarded base

Three strikes: the batter is out.

Four balls: the batter is "walked."

If the batter swings and misses it will count as a strike. A ball hit into foul territory will also be considered a strike — except if it happens on the third strike. On the third strike a hit into foul territory is ignored, unless it is caught before it touches the ground for an out.

If the pitcher throws four pitches outside of the strike zone, at which the batter does not swing, the batter will be walked, meaning he will advance to first base.

If the batter hits the ball, what happens next depends on where the ball goes and what happens to the ball when it gets there.

The strike zone

The strike zone is an area in space over home plate. If a pitch passes through the strike zone, it's a strike. If it misses the strike zone, and the batter does not swing at it, it's a ball.

Strike zone

Basics	# Batting

Batters come to bat according to the "batting order" — a sequence of players established by the team's manager at the beginning of the game. The batting order (also called the "lineup") is a significant part of the team's strategy. Stronger and weaker batters are arranged with purpose.

At bat, a batter will try to hit the pitch into fair territory. He may choose to swing at a pitch or not swing. If the ball is hit, the batter becomes a runner and will try to safely run to first base or beyond. Runners in front of him, if any, may also run — or will be forced to run because the batter needs that base.

Example: If the batter gets a hit that sends him to first base, a runner on first base is forced to run to second.

Sacrifice

While typically a batter's objective will be to safely reach a base, at times the batter's goal may be to advance a teammate already on base — even if it means putting himself out on the play.

If the ball is hit, several things may happen:

- **Safe on base:** the batter may safely reach first base or beyond.
- **Awarded bases:** the batter and possibly the runners, for a number of reasons, may be awarded one or more bases.
- **Out:** the batter or another runner may be put out by the fielders.
- **Foul:** the ball may go into foul territory.

Safe on base

By hitting the ball into fair territory, uncaught, the batter becomes a runner. If he reaches first base, or any base beyond, he will be safe as long as he is touching that base.

Awarded bases

A batter may be awarded one, two, or three bases, for a number of reasons. For example, he may be "walked" (see the next page), or he may be hit by a pitch, allowing him to advance to first base. Or he may hit a ball that bounces out of the playing field, receiving an award of two bases. Alternatively a fielder may commit a violation of the rules by obstructing the batter as he tries to advance, in which case the umpire will determine the number of bases awarded. Awarded bases are discussed in the Batting chapter.

A home run. If the batter hits the ball over the wall in fair territory, he may freely run all the way home to score. Any other runners on base will score as well.

Basics	Batting	continued

How to be put out

After the batter hits the ball, there are a several ways he or his teammates can be put out:

1. If a fielder catches the ball before it touches the ground, in fair or foul territory — or even in the stands — the batter will be out.

2. The batter or another runner will be out if a fielder catches the ball in fair territory, after it touches the ground, and if while in possession of the ball the fielder does any of the following:

- tags the batter with the ball before the batter reaches his base.

- tags first base (by stepping on it while holding the ball).

- tags out another runner with the ball, while that runner is running between bases.

- tags a base to which another runner is forced to run.

Or that fielder can throw the ball to another fielder, who will make an out as described above.

Double plays and triple plays

A double play or a triple play takes place when two or three runners are put out on a play.

Walks

After three strikes the batter will be out. After four balls the batter is considered "walked" — he will be awarded a base. This means the batter will be allowed to freely advance to first base. If there is already a runner at first base, that runner will freely advance to second, and so on. If there are runners on first, second, and third when the batter was walked, the runner from third will freely advance to home plate to score.

Fair or foul

With 0 or 1 strike in the count, if the batter hits a ball that lands in foul territory it will count as a strike. If there are already two strikes in the count, a hit that lands in foul territory will be ignored.

A hit ball that is caught in foul territory before it touches the ground, however, will be an out.

Examples: Fair Balls

Examples: Foul Balls

Basics	# Running

A runner's goal is to keep advancing bases without being put out, until he reaches home to score. While the ball is in play, a runner can be put out whenever he is not touching his base. A runner can be put out in many other ways as well. He can be called out because he missed touching a base as he was running. Or he may have misbehaved by interfering with a fielder making a play. The many ways a runner can be put out during his journey around the bases are discussed in detail in the Running chapter.

Stealing a base

Instead of waiting for a batter to get a hit, a runner can "steal" a base by running to it while the pitcher is making his pitch. Stealing a base is risky. If the runner isn't fast enough he can be put out. A runner may also be "picked off" the base to be put out. A runner will commonly take a lead off of his base, standing several feet away from the base in the direction of the next base. If the pitcher is alert he can throw to that base before the runner has a chance to return. He cannot do this, however, after he has started his pitching motion.

The pitcher or the catcher typically makes the throw to a base to catch a runner who is stealing. They therefore need to constantly monitor the runners.

Example: **Stealing a base**

Taking a lead: The runner takes a lead off his base while the pitcher is preoccupied with the batter.

Stealing a base: The runner tries to reach the base he is stealing before the catcher's throw reaches the fielder and the fielder can tag him out.

Tagging up

If a ball hit fair or foul is caught on a fly for an out, a runner may still try to reach the next base — as long as he touches his original base after the ball is caught for the out. If a runner took a lead off of his base to get a head start on his run, he must retreat to touch his base before advancing.

Example: **Tagging up**

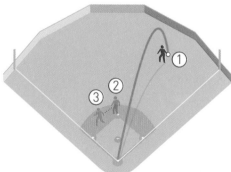

1. The ball is hit and the right fielder catches it on a fly, putting the batter out.

2. The runner waits until the fielder touches the ball before leaving his base.

3. He can now attempt to reach the next base, hopefully before a fielder can tag him with the ball to put him out.

Basics | # Running

continued

Scoring a run

One run scores every time a runner safely reaches home plate — the base from which he started when batting. On becoming a runner, either by getting a hit or by being awarded a base, the batter needs to safely reach first, second, third, then home.

Example: **Scoring a run**

A batter gets a hit and runs safely to second base.

The following batter also gets a hit and the first batter is able to run to home plate to score a run.

Runs may or may not score on a third out

A run may not score if the runner reaches home on a play that results in the third out, ending his team's time at bat for that inning. A runner will not score when, on the third out:

- a batter hits the ball but is put out before he reaches first base.

- any runner is forced out during the play (forced to run to make room on the base for the runner behind him).

- a runner behind the scoring runner missed touching a base on the same play.

In any other situation where a runner behind a scoring runner is put out for the third out, his run will score, as long as that out is made after he reaches home.

Note: If a runner is scoring the winning run in a game (because it is the last half of the last inning of the game and his run will put his team ahead), the batter in that play must also touch first base. He cannot give up running because he thinks his team has already won.

Basics	# Fielding

Fielders may put out the batter by catching a hit ball before it touches the ground. A fielder holding the ball may put out a runner, including a batter running to first, by tagging him with the ball, or by tagging the base to which he is "forced" to advance.

When a batter gets a hit he is forced to run to first base. If there is a runner already on first base, that runner is forced to run to second. Other runners are similarly forced to run if they need to vacate their base for a forced runner directly behind them.

Example: Catching a hit

The batter hits a fly ball. A fielder catches it before it touches the ground. The batter is out.

Example: Tagging the player

The batter hits a ground ball and must run to first base. A fielder can put him out by tagging him with the ball before he reaches the base.

Example: Tagging the base

Instead of tagging the batter, a fielder with the ball can tag first base by stepping on the base before the batter reaches it.

Example: Force play

With runners on first and second bases, the batter hits a ground ball toward third base. The batter and runners are forced to run.

The third baseman, holding the ball, touches (tags) third base before the runner reaches it, putting the runner out.

Explanation: Since the runner is forced to run, the fielder only needs to tag the base to put the runner out.

Example: Double play

With a runner on first base, the batter hits the ball, forcing that runner to run to second base.

After forcing out the runner at second base by tagging the base, the second baseman throws the ball to the first baseman.

The first baseman catches the ball and tags first base before the batter reaches it, putting the batter out for a double play — two outs.

Basics	The Length of the Game

Games are nine innings long

A game typically lasts for nine innings. The winning team will be the team with the most runs at the end of the ninth inning. More specifically, the game will conclude in the ninth inning when:

- either the home team or the visiting team is ahead in the score at the conclusion of the ninth inning.

- the home team is ahead in the score, either at the start of the ninth

inning or anytime during that inning. In the latter case, the game will end as soon as the winning run scores.

If the score is tied or if the visiting team is ahead in the middle of the ninth inning

If, when the home team comes to bat in the ninth inning, (they always bat in the second half of an inning), and the score is tied or the visiting team is ahead, the inning will

end as soon as the home team takes the lead. The game will be over when the winning run reaches home plate. Even if other runners can score on that last play, the home team will only win by one run — the run that puts them ahead ends the game. However, if the game ends with a winning home run, the batter and any runners on base at the time will score, and the home team may win by more than one run.

Scoreboard showing the home team winning in the ninth inning

	1	2	3	4	5	6	7	8	9
VISITING TEAM	0	1	0	1	0	0	0	0	0
HOME TEAM	0	0	1	2	0	0	1	0	-

Because the home team is ahead by a score of 4 to 2 when the visiting team completes their turn at bat in the ninth inning, there is no need for the home team to come to bat. The game is over and they win.

Basics	Extra Innings

Winning the game if the score is tied after nine innings

Baseball games cannot end in a tie, unless the game must be "called" (prematurely ended by the umpire) because weather or other factors make further play impossible. In most cases the game will continue into extra innings. The game continues until:

- the visiting team is ahead in the score at the end of the inning (after the home team concludes their time at bat), or

- the home team pulls ahead in the score.

Scoring in an extra inning is treated like the ninth inning — if the home team scores a run to take the lead, the game will end

as soon as the runner reaches home plate, winning by one run. If the game ends with a home run, the batter and all runners will score.

Therefore, if the visiting team is ahead when they complete their half of the ninth inning, or their half of an extra inning, the home team will have a chance to catch up.

An Example of a Half-Inning

Below is an example of one-half of an inning, showing a team's time at bat, and concluding when they make their third out.

1. The first batter comes to bat and is struck out (receives three strikes). **One out.**

2. The next batter is walked and advances to first base.

3. The third batter flies out. The runner remains on first base. **Two outs.**

4. The fourth batter gets a hit and goes to first base, forcing the runner to second base.

5. The fifth batter hits a line drive deep into the outfield. The ball touches the ground.

6. The runner from second base scores. The runner from first base goes to third, and the batter goes to second. **One run scores.**

7. The sixth batter grounds the ball toward the shortstop.

8. The shortstop throws the ball to the first baseman, who steps on the base for a force out. **Three outs, and the inning is over.**

Regulation games

A game will only count as an official "regulation game" if at least half of the game has been played. Basically this occurs when the losing team has completed five or more innings. See Regulation Games on page 190 for more details.

2 | Teams and Leagues

Major League Baseball oversees two leagues - the American League and the National League. This chapter discusses how teams play their many games throughout the regular season, and into the Division Championships, League Championships, and the World Series.

The leagues abide by an agreement with the Major League Baseball called the Major League Constitution. Selected items from that agreement are included in this chapter.

Teams and Leagues: contents

Teams and Leagues: Basics

Major League Baseball consists of two leagues: the American League and the National League. The leagues play under an agreement called the Major League Constitution.

page 22

The Regular Season

The regular season lasts six months, beginning late March or early April, and ending early October.

page 23

The All-Star Game

A midseason All-Star Game is played between the American League and the National League, with players chosen from each Major League Baseball team.

page 24

Postseason Championships

Teams with the most wins advance to the playoffs. The playoffs begin with the Division Series, then advance to the League Championships (the "Pennant"), and finally the World Series.

page 24

Minor League vs. Major League Rules

Several differences exist in the rules for Minor League teams.

page 27

Teams and Leagues: Basics

Overview: Major League Baseball is the organization that controls the two professional baseball leagues in North America — the American League and the National League. The two leagues encompass thirty teams — fourteen in the American League and sixteen in the National League. Both leagues divide their teams into three divisions: East, Central, and West.

Established in 1876, the National League predates the American League by twenty-four years. At it's founding it included eight teams. The American League also consisted of eight teams when it was established in 1900. Major League Baseball brought the two leagues together in 1920.

The American League consists of fourteen teams

East	Central	West
Baltimore Orioles	Chicago White Sox	Anaheim Angels
Boston Red Sox	Cleveland Indians	Oakland Athletics
New York Yankees	Detroit Tigers	Seattle Mariners
Tampa Bay Devil Rays	Kansas City Royals	Texas Rangers
Toronto Blue Jays	Minnesota Twins	

The National League consists of sixteen teams

East	Central	West
Atlanta Braves	Chicago Cubs	Arizona Diamondbacks
Florida Marlins	Cincinnati Reds	Colorado Rockies
New York Mets	Houston Astros	Los Angeles Dodgers
Philadelphia Phillies	Milwaukee Brewers	San Diego Padres
Washington Nationals	Pittsburgh Pirates	San Francisco Giants
	St. Louis Cardinals	

Basics | The Major League Constitution

Major League Baseball's agreement with the two leagues is called the Major League Constitution. This agreement covers topics ranging from the number of games played, to minimum salaries for players, to treatment programs and penalties for the use of steroids and other drugs. Many of the items discussed in this chapter come from the Major League Constitution, not the Official Rules of Major League Baseball.

The team's roster

Major League Baseball requires that each team maintain an active roster that includes a minimum of twenty-four and a maximum of twenty-five players from opening day through August 31st. If that number drops below twenty-four, due to unforeseen events, the team is required to bring that number back up to twenty-four within forty-eight hours.

The Regular Season

Overview: Baseball starts the year with spring training and preseason games. The regular season runs from late March or early April to October. Postseason championship games take place in October: the Division Series, the League Championships (the "Pennant") and the World Series. The regular season is discussed here.

162 games

The "regular season" (also called the championship season) is Major League Baseball's term for the games that lead to the Division Series Championships in October. During the regular season each team plays 162 games. The season lasts from 178 to 183 days — up to half of a year. Opening day typically takes place in early April. The final game of the regular season takes place in early October, when the postseason playoff games begin.

As an effort to spur interest in baseball worldwide, since 1996 some regular season games have been scheduled to take place outside the United States and Canada. Venues have included Puerto Rico, Mexico, and Japan. When an opening-day game is scheduled as an "international opener," in Japan for instance, the opening game may be scheduled earlier in the season — possibly in late March. When this is the case, the 183-day limit may be extended.

2,430 games

An incredible number of games take place in the regular season. Each of the thirty Major League teams plays 162 games, not including preseason or postseason games, or the All-Star Game.

162 games played by 30 teams = 2,430 games in the regular season

Games between American League and National League teams

Historically, American and National League teams would not face each other until the World Series championship at the end of the season, when the pennant winning teams from each of the leagues vie for the World Series title. That changed in 1997, when games in the regular season were scheduled between teams from the two leagues. Of 162 games scheduled for each team in the regular season, up to 18 may be inter-league games. When an inter-league game takes place, the rules of the home team's league will be followed.

Spring training and preseason games

Baseball activities begin in February and March with the start of spring training. Preseason exhibition games take place throughout March and lead right up to opening day.

The All-Star Game

Overview: The All-Star Game is an exhibition game played in the middle of the regular season. The American League plays the National League, with players chosen from every team.

The American League vs. The National League

At approximately midseason, sometime in mid-July, Major League Baseball stages the All-Star game. This is an exhibition game between American League and National League teams composed of players selected by fans. Starting players are selected by vote. At least one player from each team will be included in the game.

The "fan vote" process, of course, raises the question as to whether the selected players are the best in baseball, or simply the most popular.

The winning league gets home-field advantage at the World Series

Beginning in 2003, to give the All-Star Game more purpose, Major League Baseball declared that the winning league will be given home-field advantage in the World Series. That is, of the two teams participating in the World Series, the team whose league won the All-Star Game will have four of the seven World Series games scheduled to take place at their ballpark.

Postseason Championships

Overview: Two postseason playoffs take place prior to the World Series: the Division Series and the League Championship Series (the "Pennant").

Postseason | Division Series

Four winning teams, and a "wild card"

Each Division Series is a best-of-five-game event. As implied by its name, it puts teams with the best win-loss records from each division in competition. This means that, within each league, one team each from the East, Central, and West divisions will compete. A fourth team is also selected — the *wild card* team. To select the wild card team:

1. The teams with the second best win-loss percentage are identified in each division.

2. Of these three teams, the one with the best win-loss percentage is chosen.

Note: The win-loss percentage is simply the number of games won divided by the total number of games played (the total number of games played is 162 at the end of the regular season).

Four teams will enter the Division Series

Within each league, four teams pair off to compete in two separate Division Series. The four teams divide into pairs according to the following rules:

- the team with the highest win-loss percentage will play the team with the lowest win-loss percentage.

- if this places two teams from the same division against each other, the pairs will be rearranged — the team with the highest win-loss record will play the team with the second-to-lowest win-loss record.

Two teams will advance in each league

The two winning teams in each league will advance to play each other for the League Championship.

Division Series: The selection process is the same for the American and the National leagues. Using the National League as an example, if at the end of the regular season the two teams with the highest win-loss percentage in each geographic division are:

East	Wins	Losses	Win-Loss Percentage
1. Atlanta Braves	96	66	.593
2. Philadelphia Phillies	86	76	.531
Central			
1. St. Louis Cardinals	105	57	.648
2. Houston Astros	92	70	.568
West			
1. Los Angeles Dodgers	93	69	.574
2. San Francisco Giants	91	71	.562

The Atlanta Braves, St. Louis Cardinals, and Los Angeles Dodgers ended the regular season with the best records in their division, so they will participate in the Division Series. Of the three second-place teams, the Houston Astros have the best record, making them the wild card. The Astros will become the fourth team to play.

Of these four teams, the St. Louis Cardinals have the highest win-loss percentage (.648), and the Houston Astros have the lowest (.568). However, because they are in the same division, they will not play each other. The Cardinals will play the Dodgers, who have the second-to-lowest record. The Braves will play the Astros.

Home-field advantage

Since the Division Series is a best-of-five game set, the series ends as soon as one team wins three games. Three of the five games will be scheduled to take place at the home of the team with the highest win-loss percentage, giving that team the home-field advantage. Games one, two, and five will be played at their stadium. If the series goes to five games, they will have the advantage of playing three of the games in their own ballpark.

Postseason | League Championship Series (Pennant)

Each league next holds a League Championship Series (the "Pennant"), to be played by the two winning teams from the Division Series. This is a best-of-seven game series. In scheduling the games, the home-field advantage will be given to the team that had the highest win-loss percentage in the regular season. That team will be scheduled to host games one, two, six, and seven.

In each League Championship Series, the first team to win four games will win the pennant.

Postseason | The World Series

The World Series places the winners of the American League Championship Series and the National League Championship Series in competition. The World Series is a best-of-seven game series. The home field advantage for the World Series goes to the team whose league won the All-Star Game. That team will host games one, two, six, and seven. In addition to the notoriety of becoming World Series champions, the winning team receives a World Series trophy, and its players receive World Series rings.

Postseason	Steps to the World Series: Example

The Regular Season

162 games

In the regular season, each teams plays 162 games, vying for a place in their league's Division Series.

The Division Series

Best of five games

Within each league, the teams with the highest win-loss percentage in each division will advance.

So will a fourth "wild card" team, the team with the next-best record.

The four teams will pair off, creating two different Division Series per league. A team needs to win three out of five games.

The League Championship

Best of seven games

Also known as "the Pennant," the two winning teams from the Division Series will play each other A team needs to win four out of seven games.

The World Series

Best of seven games

The team that wins the American League pennant will play the National League's pennant winner in the World Series. Four out of seven World Series games must be won to become the World Series champions.

Example: This diagram shows steps to the World Series, using the National League as an example. The American League's process is identical.

The National League

Major vs. Minor League rules

Overview: The Official Rules of Major League Baseball point out several differences between rules used in the Major and the Minor Leagues.

Differences are:

1. Helmets must have double ear flaps: Minor League players are required to use double ear flap helmets, protecting both ears. Major League players may use single ear flap helmets, protecting only the ear that faces the pitcher.

2. When double headers are scheduled: the Minor League may limit each game to seven innings. In this case, rules that typically apply to the ninth inning will apply to the seventh inning. For example, because the seventh inning is now the last scheduled inning of the game, the game will end at the conclusion of the first half of the seventh inning when the home team (who always bats after the visiting team) is in the lead, or end as soon as the home team pulls ahead in that inning.

3. Rules regarding suspended and terminated games: When weather or other factors make further play impossible, the Major League allows games to terminate in a tie score or a "no game."

The Minor League calls for these games to be suspended. Play will resume on another day. (See page 191 for more information.)

4. Requirements for the individual pitching championship: At the end of the season each league names an individual pitching champion, the pitcher with the best earned run average (ERA).

The Major League requires the selected pitcher to have pitched the number of innings equal to or greater than the total number of games played in the season (162 innings or more).

The Minor League requires their pitchers to have pitched only 80 percent of the number of games (.80 x 144 games in the Minor League season = 115 innings or more).

Note: The Minor League is also known as the National Association, the term used in the Official Rules of Major League Baseball. To avoid any confusion between the terms National Association and National League, we are using the term Minor League in our discussions of the rules.

3 | Before the Game Starts

Although the game officially starts when the umpire calls "play," the rules require a number of activities to take place beforehand. These range from the home team's manager determining if the game will take place due to weather, to the exchange of batting orders that will lock in the sequence by which players will come to bat.

Before the Game Starts: contents

Before the Game Starts

Overview: Before the game, umpires need to make sure the field and the equipment being used meet the specifications laid out in the rules.

Umpire's tasks before the game starts

Before the game begins the umpire is responsible for checking the equipment used in the game. The official rules of baseball require that gloves be within specific size limits, that bats and balls conform to official standards, and that uniforms meet certain requirements. The umpire is responsible for ensuring that:

- bats, balls, uniforms, and gloves meet specifications.

- the white lines marking the field are correct and intact. Lines must be in place to indicate:

  - baselines
  - foul lines
  - the batter's box
  - the catcher's box
  - the coaches' boxes

- the pitcher's mound and pitcher's plate are correct.

- he receives the game's supply of baseballs, provided by the home team. The baseballs need to meet the specifications of Major League Baseball.

- there are at least a dozen more baseballs available for use in the game if required.

- he has at least two baseballs in his possession to be put into the game when:

  - a batter hits the ball into the stands or somewhere else out of play.

  - the ball is worn out or otherwise unacceptable for use — for instance, because it has become discolored, scratched, or frayed.

  - the pitcher asks for a new ball to be put into play.

Weather and field conditions

Before the start of the game the home team manager is in charge of the field. This means he decides if weather or poor field conditions will be cause for the game to be delayed or rescheduled for another day.

When a manager or umpire is in charge of the field it means he is also in charge of the ground crew and field assistants. If field conditions need to be improved, the manager (before the game) or the umpire-in-chief (during the game) is responsible for the maintenance activities.

Just before the game, and throughout the remainder of the game, the umpire-in-chief takes authority. He assumes this responsibility as soon as the home team manager hands the batting order to the umpire-in-chief several minutes before the game's start.

Double-headers

The umpire-in-chief remains in charge between games in a double-header. He becomes the sole judge concerning whether or not the second game of a double-header should be delayed or rescheduled.

Toward the end of the season

If a home team manager decides to postpone a game, or decides not to, the visiting team may appeal this decision to the league president, asking him to override the home team manager's authority to decide whether or not to start the game — on the basis that home team manager's decision could be biased. Alternately, each league may relieve all its managers of this authority in the closing weeks of the season, automatically transferring this authority to the league president for each game.

Thirty Minutes Before

Each team must identify its manager.

Each team is required to identify a manager at least thirty minutes prior to the start of the game. Although not common practice, the manager may also be a player on the team. The manager has many responsibilities identified in the rules. However, he may delegate some of his responsibilities to his coaching staff. If he does, he will notify the umpire sometime before the start of the game that, in specific situations, a coach will be acting on his behalf.

Team members cannot mingle.

Players in uniform are not allowed in the stands before the game. The rules prohibit managers, coaches, or players from interacting with spectators or members of the opposing team, before or during the game.

Preparing the Baseballs

Overview: Behind the scenes, the umpire must inspect each of the many baseballs supplied for the game. He also plays with mud.

The home team supplies the umpire with a large supply of baseballs for each game. This can total sixty baseballs or more. The balls must be delivered in sealed boxes, with the seals intact. Each package displays the signature of the league president. On receiving the baseballs an umpire inspects and prepares each one. This entails removing the gloss from the new ball by rubbing it with a special type of mud.

Lena Blackburne Rubbing Mud

The rules require the umpire, on opening each sealed package containing a baseball, to inspect the baseball and to "remove its gloss." This, by tradition, is accomplished by rubbing each ball with mud.

Since the 1930s, umpires have been using a very specific type of mud. In the 1910s and 1920s, Russell Aubrey "Lena" Blackburne played infield for the Chicago White Sox. He later was hired as the third-base coach for the Philadelphia Athletics. In previous years umpires used a variety of substances to remove the shine from baseballs. In 1938, Lena came across something that was perfect. Somewhere in New Jersey, at an undisclosed location along the Delaware River, he found a fine, chocolate-pudding-like mud. The mud could be rubbed on a baseball, removing the gloss without discoloring it or otherwise affecting the ball. It worked perfectly. Within a few years every American League team was using it, and by the late 1950s, every team in the National League as well.

Lena Blackburne Rubbing Mud is still being collected from the banks of the Delaware River and is used by every major league umpire today.

new ball

gloss removed

Forfeits

Overview: Teams can win or lose even before the game starts. A team can forfeit a game — a situation in which the umpire-in-chief, as penalty for a team's flagrant violation of the rules, can award the game to the opposing team. Forfeited games are automatically assigned a score of 0 to 9.

A game can be over before it even starts.

The following are causes that will lead to forfeiture of the game, possibly before a first pitch is even thrown.

1. Unfit field conditions. If the umpire-in-chief determines the field is not in proper playing condition, he can call a forfeit in favor of the visiting team.

2. The home team's failure to provide police protection for the field. If one or more fans come onto the field, interfering with players or the play, the visiting team may refuse to play until the fan or fans have been ejected. The home team will be allowed at least fifteen minutes, possibly more, for police or security personnel to clear the field. If not cleared, at any point after the fifteen-minute period the umpire may declare a forfeit in favor of the visiting team.

3. A team does not enter the field, or they refuse to start the game within five minutes of the call of "play" by the umpire-in-chief. If the delay is due to a reason that cannot be avoided, the umpire may forgive the delay.

4. A team fails to show up on the field for game two of a double-header following the twenty-minute interval normally scheduled between the games (unless the interval that day has been extended).

5. A team tries deliberately to delay the game or to shorten the game's duration.

6. A team refuses, or is unable to place nine players on the field .

A forfeit of a game must be called by the umpire-in-chief. He is the sole decision maker on forfeits.

Five Minutes Before

The umpire-in-chief will enter the field five minutes prior to the start of the game and proceed to home plate, where:

- the home team manager hands two identical copies of the home team's batting order to the umpire.

- the visiting team's manager hands two identical copies of the visiting team's batting order to the umpire.

- the umpire checks both lists to make sure they are identical, and looks for obvious mistakes.

- on delivering the lists to the umpire, the batting orders are established for the entire game, and substitutions can only be made as provided by the rules.

While the list handed to the umpire establishes the batting order for the game, the teams are not bound by obvious unintentional errors or omissions. For instance, if the list contains only eight names instead

of nine, or if it shows two players with identical names without identifying which player was intended, the error should simply be corrected. The team's manager or captain should be notified of the error and the team will be allowed to correct it prior to the start of the game.

- confirming that the lists are identical and with no mistakes detected, the umpire retains one copy of each list and hands the opposing team's list to each manager.

- The umpires assume their authority over the game and the field. This means the umpire-in-chief now has the authority to suspend or postpone a game due to poor weather or unfit conditions of the field, and to determine when and if a game will be resumed.

Note: If a designated hitter will come to bat in place of the pitcher, that

designated hitter must be identified in the batting order handed to the umpire-in-chief Although either league is free to adopt the rule allowing designated hitters, only the American League is using it.

Ground rules

Each ballpark has it's own set of ground rules covering issues specific to that field. Ground rules are specific to the current game and stadium, and address situations not covered in the official rule book. Rules range from balls getting trapped under rolls of tarp, to the use of retractable roofs. The manager of the home team may wish to impose other special ground rules prior to the start of the game. If the visiting team's manager agrees, the ground rules will go into effect. If not, the umpire may impose his own ground rules to cover special circumstances associated with the game that day.

The visiting team wears darker uniforms and always bats first.

If you are sitting in a stadium there should be no confusion over which team is the visiting team — just read the logos on the uniforms. If glancing at a game on television, however, it's easy to quickly identify the home team and visiting team.

Each team owns two sets of uniforms — one set is white and the other darker — a light gray or beige. The home team wears white. The visiting team's uniforms will be darker. In every game, the visiting team comes to bat first.

Home team

Visiting team

Starting the Game

The starting pitcher

The batting order names a starting pitcher who will be required to pitch to at least one batter. The starting pitcher, unless he becomes sick or injured, making him unable to pitch, must pitch at least until the first batter completes his turn at bat — by reaching a base or by being put out.

At the start of the game:

- **The nine members of the home team take their position on the field.** This means eight players, including the pitcher, will be in fair territory. The catcher will take his position in the catcher's box, behind home plate — therefore the only fielder not stationed in fair territory.

- **The pitcher will complete his warm-up pitches.** The pitcher is allowed up to eight warm-up pitches, not to exceed one minute. However, if there are delays in the game for other reasons — including a commercial break if the game is being televised, the umpires may be lenient on this rule.

- **The first batter in the visiting team's batting order takes his position in the batter's box.** He must be in position when the pitcher starts his pitch (see the Batting chapter for information on the batting box, page 90).

- **The first and third-base coaches will be in their positions.** The base coaches are the two members of the offensive team who, in addition to the starting batter, will take their positions at the start of the game. The coaches boxes are located fifteen feet to the sides of first base and third base (see The Manager and Coaches chapter, page 158).

- **The umpire will call "play."** On this call the ball becomes live (or "in play") and the game has officially started.

- **The pitcher will deliver his first pitch,** which must be thrown within twenty seconds of the call of "play."

Of the nine fielders, only the pitcher and the catcher have defined locations. The other seven fielders may position themselves anywhere in fair territory. Their "typical" positions are not required by the rules — but make perfect sense if the team is going to adequately cover the field.

Restarting a suspended or a protested game

If the game being played is actually the remainder of a game from a previous day that was suspended because of rain or other reasons, the game will resume from the point at which the game was suspended. The next batter, the fielders and batting order will be the same — although player substitutions may be made as provided in the official rules.

Teams can protest a game to the league president if they believe the umpire made a crucial decision in error, one that may have affected the outcome of the game. The umpire's call may not have been in accordance with the official rules of baseball. If the league president sides with the protest, the game will be rescheduled. The game will be replayed, starting from the play in which the protested call was made.

For more on protested games see pages 145 and 164.

4 | Equipment

Baseball equipment is strictly regulated under the rules. Every bat must be a solid piece of wood (no cork allowed), and the size and weight tolerances of each Major League baseball are specified.

This chapter will discuss equipment dimensions and specifications.

Equipment: contents

The Ball

Overview: Although the official rules cover the basic specifications for the baseball, they go into remarkably little detail. However, all baseballs used in the Major Leagues are made by one manufacturer, by hand, with exacting specifications and consistency.

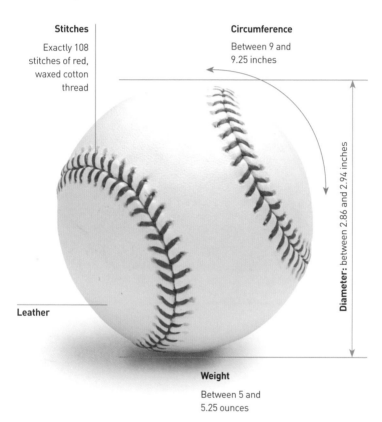

Stitches
Exactly 108 stitches of red, waxed cotton thread

Circumference
Between 9 and 9.25 inches

Diameter: between 2.86 and 2.94 inches

Leather

Weight
Between 5 and 5.25 ounces

Layers and construction

The core		Outer layers
Red rubber outer layer		White horsehide or cowhide
Black rubber inner layer		Cotton winding
Rubber and cork core		4-ply gray wool
		3-ply white wool
		4-ply gray wool

The Bat

Overview: The official rules concerning bats begin, "The bat must be a smooth round stick...."

2.75 inches at its widest point

No longer than 42 inches

18 inch handle area

One solid piece of wood

While college baseball allows metal bats, the Major Leagues will only allow one-piece wood bats.

The rules state that no laminated or experimental bat can be used unless it has been cleared by the Rules Committee.

The handle

The handle area can be treated with any substance or material to improve the grip. Typically, pine tar is used for this purpose, applied to the bat with a rag.

Whatever material is used, it may not extend more than eighteen inches from the bottom end, or the bat will be removed from the game.

If a bat that has already been used in a game is discovered to have broken the eighteen-inch rule, it will not be grounds for ejecting or even calling the batter out.

Note: Since home plate is seventeen inches wide, umpires will often check pine tar on a bat handle by measuring it against the plate.

Cupped bats

It's permitted to make an indentation at the head of the bat. This is called a cupped bat or a teacup bat. It must be a curved indentation no deeper than one inch and between one and two inches in diameter. It should never contain a foreign substance.

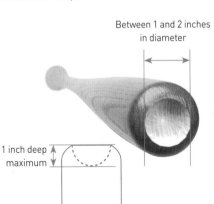

Between 1 and 2 inches in diameter

1 inch deep maximum

Gloves and Mitts: Basic Anatomy

Overview: The following shows basic terms and requirements that are applied to all gloves and mitts. In the next pages we will discuss the measurements for each specific glove or mitt.

The Crotch

This is the term for the area between the thumb and index finger. It is where the web sits.

Measurements

The measurements listed in the rules are taken by placing a tape measure directly against the surface, measuring every contour of the glove or mitt.

Mitts vs. gloves

Mitts are generally larger than gloves and have a single area for all the fingers (like a mitten). Mitts can only be used by the catcher and the first baseman.

A glove has individual finger sections and can be used by all other fielders, however, there are a few more constraints applied to the pitcher's glove.

If the glove fits....

The size of the glove depends both on the a player's preference as well as the rules. Most shortstops and second baseman like a smaller glove so they can catch and throw quickly. Outfielders typically like bigger gloves to make the catch a bit easier. Pitchers like a bigger glove with closed webbing to hide the ball from the view of the batter.

The Web

The web must be secured and constrained completely on all sides including the top. If the lacing stretches or becomes loose, it must be repaired to meet the proper requirements.

Palm

Weight

While there are strict size and material limitations, there are no weight requirements for gloves or mitts.

Base or heel

Webbing variation

The webbing can be constructed in a number of different ways. In all cases, the web must control and limit the space between the thumb and fingers. A web that is constructed to expand or give like a net is not allowed. The idea is to make the glove flexible without allowing it to expand to "net" or "trap" the ball.

Catcher's Mitt

Overview: The catcher's mitt is allowed to be bigger than any other type of glove. The design of this glove has evolved over the years to handle everything from 100 m.p.h fastballs to awkward and unpredictable knuckleballs.

Reinforced web

A catcher's mitt is typically reinforced in the webbing and padded through the palm.

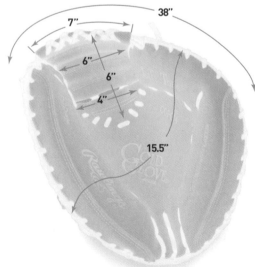

Maximum dimensions

The mitt must not exceed the following dimensions:

Overall height	**15.5"**
Circumference	**38"**
Top edge of web	**7"**
Web height	**6"**
Top web width	**6"**
Bottom web width	**4"**

First Baseman's Mitt

Overview: The first baseman uses a mitt with larger webbing than other fielder's gloves. In a typical game, the first baseman will catch more balls than anyone aside from the catcher and pitcher.

Leather tubes

This typical style of webbing is constructed out of a lattice of leather tubes threaded together with leather lacing.

Maximum dimensions

The mitt must not exceed the following dimensions:

Overall height	**12"**
Palm width	**8"**
Web height	**5"**
Top web width	**4"**
Bottom web width	**3.5"**

Fielder's Glove

Overview: Every player except the catcher and first baseman can wear a glove that falls within these specifications. While maximum dimensions are shown, infielders other than the first baseman typically prefer smaller, "faster" gloves.

Maximum dimensions

The glove must not exceed the following dimensions:

Overall height	**12"**
Palm width	**7.75"**
Web height	**5.75"**
Top web width	**4.5"**
Bottom web width. . . .	**3.5"**

Pitcher's Glove

Overview: The pitcher's glove must conform to the same specifications as a fielder's, but it must be uniform in color to minimize distractions to the batter. It cannot be white or gray or a color that may hide the ball.

Uniform color

The rules specify that the pitcher's glove should not be multiple colors, including the stitching, lacing, and webbing. Presumably, a glove with overly distracting coloration would have to be removed. In reality, many gloves include some color variation (like the one shown).

The pitcher may not attach a foreign material of another color to his glove.

Bigger is better

Pitchers typically like big gloves with closed webbing (as shown) to help them hide the ball from the batter.

Maximum dimensions

The pitcher's glove dimensions are the same as those for a fielder's glove:

Overall height	**12"**
Palm width	**7.75"**
Web height	**5.75"**
Top web width	**4.5"**
Bottom web width. . . .	**3.5"**

The Uniforms

Overview: All team members must wear matching uniforms, identical in the style, colors, trim, and graphics.

Home and visiting team colors

Every team must have two sets of uniforms. A white uniform is worn for home games, and a uniform of a distinctly darker color must be worn for away games.

Player identification

The number of each player must be on his back in letters that are at least six inches tall.

The rules state that each league can create guidelines for displaying a player's name on their uniform. Typically, players have their last name printed on their back. The rules note that a name other than the player's last name (like a nickname) may be used by permission of the league president.

Commercialization

Company logos, patches, and labels for the purpose of commercial promotion are not allowed on the uniforms.

Labels and logos on the equipment must be reasonably small and not overly prominent.

Distractions

Players must never attach items to their uniform that differ in color or that may prove distracting. Shiny buttons or details are illegal for the same reason.

No one can wear a graphic or a detail of clothing that depicts or resembles a baseball "to prevent players from ever seeing more than one baseball at a time on the field."

Example: A uniform of the 1955 New York Giants worn by Willie Mays.

Sleeves

Sleeve lengths can vary according to a player's preference as long as both sleeves are the same length and they are not frayed, ragged, or slit.

Caps

Every player has one, fans all over the world wear them, but the rules don't mention them.

Undershirts

Undershirts can be exposed and can have logos, letters or numbers on the sleeves, but they must be a solid color and the same color for everyone on the team.

Note: The pitcher's undershirt must not have any markings because they could distract the batters.

Evolution of the uniform

Like so many aspects of the game, the rules have changed very little over the years in regards to the uniform. This uniform of the world champion Red Sox team of 1908 would be acceptable today (according to the rules).

Helmets

Overview: The modern helmet is a hard plastic shell with foam padding inside.

Helmets are mandatory for batters, catchers, and bat or ball girls and boys while performing their duties.

If after a reasonable warning someone refuses to wear the appropriate head gear, the umpire will eject the culprit from the game. Further disciplinary action may be warranted.

Ear flaps

Helmets come with either one or two ear flaps.

Since 1982. Any player who entered the Major Leagues during or since the 1982 season must wear a helmet with either a single or double ear flap.

The Minor Leagues. All players must wear a helmet with double ear flaps.

Catcher's helmet and mask

Catchers must also wear a protective helmet while in their fielding position.

Although the rules don't mention it, catchers also wear masks to protect their faces. Some catcher's helmets come with an integrated hockey-style mask. Other more traditional models are designed to be used with a separate mask.

Shoes

Overview: For obvious safety reasons, baseball shoes cannot have pointed spikes (like golf shoes).

Plastic or metal treads

Baseball cleats are approximately one-half inch tall. They come in a variety of configurations and materials, but they must never come to a point at the bottom.

Ty Cobb

Ty Cobb, who was not known for his good sportsmanship, was said to sharpen his cleats so infielders would think twice before attempting to hold their ground as he slid into a base.

5 | Field Specifications

Baseball is a game of inches. A change in any of the critical dimensions in the infield, even by a small amount, could change the game dramatically.

While the infield dimensions are specified, outfields and foul areas vary widely. This chapter will show the specifications for the infield, including the bases and the pitcher's mound. It will also show the vast differences in sizes and shapes of outfields and foul areas at existing Major League ballparks.

Field Specifications: contents

The Field

Overview: The infield portion of all baseball fields must be identical, but the outfield can vary a great deal from one stadium to the next.

The Field | ## The Infield

Optional dimensions and specifications

Not all of the standard dimensions are mandatory. The following points are preferable but not enforced as a rule:

- Ballparks should face toward the East Northeast.

- The distance from home base to the backstop (the wall behind home plate) should be a minimum of sixty feet. The same goes for the distance between the infield foul lines and the surrounding fences or walls.

- It is up to the home ball club to decide which areas are covered by grass or dirt. The diagram shows a standard layout.

| **The Field** | # The Outfield |

Outfield requirements

There must be a minimum of 325 feet from home plate to the nearest fence, stand, or wall along the right and left field foul lines. There should be a minimum of 400 feet to the center field wall.

Fields prior to 1958

Older ball parks were more varied in dimensions, and the restrictions were looser. The current regulations only apply to fields constructed after June 1, 1958. If an existing field pre-dates that period, then the closest distance between home plate and any wall or fence in fair territory must be 250 feet.

It is "desirable" for right and left field to be at least 320 feet, and center field to be at least 400 feet.

Remodeling. Any changes made to an existing ball park should not cause the field to shrink below the minimum distances.

An endless outfield

While there are rules regarding the minimum sizes for the field, nothing prevents the outfield from extending outward from home plate indefinitely.

The Batter's Box

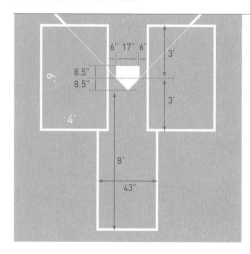

Each batter's box (one on each side of home plate) is six feet deep and four feet wide.

The catcher's box extends eight feet below the back of home plate. It's enough room for the catcher and umpire to be out of the way of the batter's swing.

The Pitcher's Mound

Overview: The pitcher's mound is ten inches tall and eighteen feet in diameter. The "rubber" (also called the pitcher's plate) is six inches by twenty four inches and is sixty feet six inches from the back (the point) of home plate.

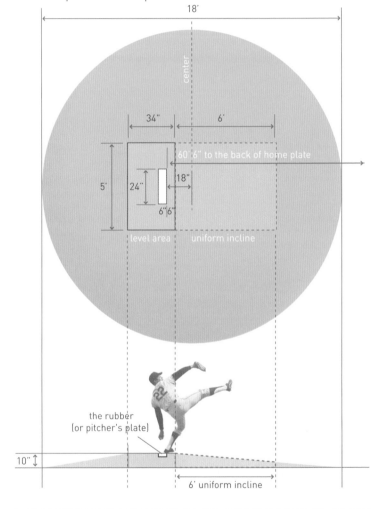

The pitcher's mound is ten inches tall, and the front of the mound is a uniform incline for six feet beyond the flattened area at the top of the mound. This uniform incline will drop one vertical inch for every horizontal foot for a distance of six feet toward home plate.

The degree of slope on all other areas of the mound is not critical and can slope gradually to field level.

The Bases

Overview: First, second, and third bases are identical squares, while home plate is an irregular five-sided shape. Each base is placed ninety feet apart. Together they describe the infield diamond.

Base placement

First and third bases are placed with their outer edges against the foul lines and baseline.

Second base is placed so that its center is on the point at which the baselines intersect.

Home plate

Home plate is fixed securely so that the bottom is flush with the ground. The edges are beveled down.

The bases are secured in place by slipping a square pipe under the base (called the "anchor") into a fitting in the ground.

Steal a base. Really.

First, second, and third bases are not fixed in place and can be easily pulled free and carried away. This was demonstrated in 2001 by Pirates manager Lloyd McClendon when he disagreed with an umpire's call. In protest, McClendon picked up first base and carried it away into the dugout after being ejected.

Major League Fields

Overview: All baseball fields must have identical infield dimensions, but the outfield and foul territory can differ greatly. In this section, you can compare the basic shapes and sizes of the current Major League stadiums.

The required dimensions

Every field must have the same specifications in the infield. Fields built after 1958 must have a minimum distance of 325 feet from home plate to the outfield wall along the left and right foul lines and a minimum of 400 feet to the center field wall. There must be no obstructions in fair territory (fences, stands or walls) closer than 250 feet from home plate. It is recommended, but not mandatory, that the foul area all the way around the infield be a minimum of 60 feet from the base lines. Aside from these specifications, every field can be designed differently.

The prototypical modern baseball field

This diagram shows a symmetrical field that meets all the Major League requirements and recommendations.

Note: Every field illustrated in this section is shown at the same scale. The dotted blue line in each diagram shows an arc drawn 250 feet from home plate for reference.

MLB Fields | # Field Comparisons

American League East

Baltimore Orioles

American League East

Tampa Bay Devil Rays

American League East

Boston Red Sox

American League East

Toronto Blue Jays

American League East

New York Yankees

American League Central

Chicago White Sox

MLB Fields | # Field Comparisons

American League Central

Cleveland Indians

American League Central

Minnesota Twins

American League Central

Detroit Tigers

American League West

Anaheim Angels

American League Central

Kansas City Royals

American League West

Oakland Athletics

MLB Fields | Field Comparisons

American League West

Seattle Mariners

American League West

Texas Rangers

National League East

Atlanta Braves

National League East

Florida Marlins

National League East

New York Mets

National League East

Philadelphia Phillies

MLB Fields | # Field Comparisons

National League East

Washington Nationals

National League Central

Houston Astros

National League Central

Chicago Cubs

National League Central

Milwaukee Brewers

National League Central

Cincinnati Reds

National League Central

Pittsburgh Pirates

MLB Fields | # Field Comparisons

National League Central
St. Louis Cardinals

National League West
Los Angeles Dodgers

National League West
Arizona Diamondbacks

National League West
San Diego Padres

National League West
Colorado Rockies

National League West
San Francisco Giants

6 | Pitching

Because he handles the ball constantly, the pitcher is perhaps the most closely scrutinized player in the game.

The rules strictly specify the movements a pitcher is and is not allowed to make when throwing the ball from the pitcher's mound. This chapter covers a wide range of topics such as balks, ball tampering (it's frowned upon), and visits to the pitcher's mound by a coach or manager.

Pitching: contents

Pitching Positions: The Windup and Set (or Stretch) Positions

Overview: There are two legal pitching positions that can be used by a pitcher at any time in a game — the windup position and the set position.

Pitching Positions	The Windup Position

The delivery from the windup position is designed to give the pitcher optimum power.

The windup is typically used when there are no runners on base. It's a slow and deliberate delivery that would allow plenty of time for a runner from first or second base to steal a base.

His head must be facing the batter.

His hands must be in front of his body.

His pivot foot (the right foot for a right-handed pitcher, left foot for a left-handed pitcher) is on the rubber, his "free foot" can be to the side or behind the plate. His body will be facing home plate.

Home plate

rubber

The windup delivery and footwork

1. To start, both feet must be on the ground. His pivot foot must be on the rubber, and his other foot can be anywhere – usually just behind his pivot foot. This is the position in which the pitcher takes his signs.

2. As he begins the pitch, his free foot can move one step back.

3. The pitcher then lifts his leg around the pivot leg, and the pivot foot will turn to be parallel with the rubber for traction.

4. The pitcher will lunge forward into the pitch.

5. After releasing the ball, he will try to be in a position to field a hit ball.

Pitching with a runner on base

The pitcher's role becomes far more complicated when there is a runner on base. Not only must he try to put the batter out, he must prevent the runner from stealing a base or taking a big lead.

Accordingly, the rules are more complex and constraining for a pitcher when there is a runner on base. He is not allowed to "deceive the runner" during his pitching sequence, or he will be charged with a balk (see page 68).

Pitching Positions

The Set Position

Pitchers use the set position to keep runners at bay by delivering the ball to the plate faster and with less warning. The delivery is a quick lunge into the pitch, and the pitcher sacrifices some power.

The set position is used primarily when there are runners on base.

His head must be facing the batter.

He must move from a position where one hand is by his side or behind him to a position where both hands are in front of his body.

With his pivot foot in contact with the rubber, his free foot must be in front of the rubber. This puts his body in a sideways position.

Home Plate

rubber

The set delivery and footwork

1. To start, both feet must be on the ground, and the entire length of his back foot must be on or against the rubber. This is the position in which the pitcher takes his signs.

2. As he moves to the set position, his feet remain in the same position.

3. As he begins the pitch, he will lift his front foot up and back quickly into an abbreviated windup.

4. From here, the two deliveries are very similar — the pitcher will lunge forward into the pitch.

5. After releasing the ball, he will try to be in a position to field a hit ball.

The Pitching Sequence: Windup vs. Set

Overview: While the rules of baseball refer to the windup and set as alternate "positions," it's easier to understand them if you consider the entire sequence and delivery of each.

The windup position: home plate is toward the right →

1. Taking signs. The pitcher stands with his pivot foot on the rubber and his other foot on or slightly behind the rubber. He will be facing home plate.

2. The windup position. The pitcher may raise his glove in front of him to indicate he is ready to pitch. Any throwing motion after this will commit the pitcher to the pitch. From this point he can:

• step off the rubber
• commit to the pitch

3. The beginning of the pitch. The pitcher takes a step back and brings his hands up over his head.

As soon as he begins this motion, the pitcher has committed to the pitch and must complete it.

The set position: home plate is toward the right →

1. Taking signs. The pitcher stands with his back foot (the pivot foot) on the rubber, and one hand behind him or at his side. He will be facing first base if he is a left-hander, or third base if he is a right-hander.

2. Optional transition. The pitcher can make a quick motion, raising his hands up or even above his head as he moves into the set position.

3. The set position. The pitcher brings his hands in front of him with both hands on the ball. He must come to a complete stop in his motion. He can remain in this position indefinitely. From this point he can:

• step off the plate
• throw to a base
• commit to the pitch

Comparison of the windup and set deliveries:

The windup is slow but powerful

- Pitcher commits to the pitch as soon as he begins his motion.
- A big slow step backward and then a powerful lunge forward into the pitch.

The set is quick and flexible

- Pitcher can decide to throw to a base or commit to the pitch at the last instant.
- Quick delivery of the ball.

4. The windup or pivot. The pitcher literally winds himself up to deliver as much power as he can, lifting his leg up and around his body.

5. The stride. The pitcher lunges toward home plate as he releases the ball.

6. The follow-through. After the pitcher releases the ball, he is typically facing the batter, ready to field a hit.

4. The beginning of the pitch. The pitcher takes a step towards the plate.

At soon as he begins this motion, the pitcher has committed to the pitch and must complete it.

5. The stride. The pitcher lunges toward home plate as he releases the ball.

6. The follow-through. After the pitcher releases the ball, he is typically facing the batter, ready to field the a hit.

The Balk

Overview: A balk is a penalty charged against a pitcher for deviating from the legal pitching motion while a runner is on base. It can occur during a pitch, or during a throw to a base to put out a base runner who has stepped off his base (called "picking off a runner.")

Since the rules are somewhat complex and extremely subtle, it can be a tricky judgment call on the part of the umpire. The umpire is instructed to ultimately base the balk charge on the "intent" of the pitcher. If he decides that the pitcher is intentionally trying to deceive a runner, he must call a balk.

Intent of the Balk. The balk is meant to prevent the pitcher from deceiving the base runner. The pitcher will occasionally try to catch a runner off guard in order to prevent possibilities such as stealing a base or getting too much of a lead off a base.

Penalty. In all cases, the penalty for a balk is a single base awarded to all runners (but not the batter). This penalty is always charged to the pitcher.

Dead ball. For a balk called while the pitcher is throwing to a base, or while he is not involved in the act of pitching, the ball is dead immediately.

On a pitched balk, it is a delayed dead ball. This means that the umpire will wait to see if the batter gets a hit before calling the balk. If he gets a hit the balk will not be called.

Quick list: eleven ways to balk

The following is a list of quick descriptions, showing at a glance the eleven ways to balk. The complete explanations begin on the next page.

1. **Make a quick pitch.** During the set position the pitcher must come to a complete stop, and he must not pitch before the batter is ready.

2. **Fail to have both hands on the ball in the set position.** A pitcher must have both hands on the ball, in front of his body.

3. **Pitch while not touching the rubber.** His pivot foot must be touching it.

4. **Pitch without looking at the batter.** A pitcher's head must be facing the batter.

5. **Fail to step toward and ahead of the throw.** He must step in the direction of the throw before making the throw.

6. **Fake a throw to first base.** Once he makes a motion to throw to first base he must complete the throw.

7. **Make a pitching motion without completing the pitch.** From the set or windup position, he cannot start to pitch without completing the pitch.

8. **Fake a pitch.** A pitcher cannot make a motion that could deceive the runner or batter.

9. **Delay of game.** This is a judgment call by the umpire, if he feels a pitcher is intentionally delaying the game.

10. **Catcher outside the catcher's box during an intentional walk.** The catcher must be in his box at the beginning of a pitch-out (intentional walk).

11. **Drop the ball.** A pitcher cannot drop the ball while on the rubber.

The Balk	# Eleven Ways to Balk

1. Make a quick pitch. If the pitcher speeds up his normal pitching motion, it's considered deceptive and the umpire must call a balk. There are two common types of quick pitches:

- Pitching before the batter is ready. For example, the pitcher cannot step off the pitcher's plate and then quickly step back on and pitch the ball, catching the batter unprepared.

- Failure to come to a complete stop during the set position. This critical pause must be a noticeable stop in the pitcher's motion.

Note: A quick pitch is illegal even if there are no base runners, at which time the penalty is a ball.

2. Fail to have both hands on the ball in the set position. While in the set position (see page 64 and 66), the pitcher must keep both hands on the ball. If he takes one hand off the ball, the umpire will call a balk.

3. Pitching while not on the rubber. The pitcher's pivot foot must be touching the rubber during a legal pitching motion. If the pitcher makes a pitch when his foot is not in contact with the rubber, it's a balk.

4. Pitch without looking at the batter. If the pitcher pitches the ball without his head turned towards the batter, it is considered deceptive (and probably a bit dangerous). A balk will be called.

5. Fail to step toward and ahead of the throw. The pitcher is required to take a clear and deliberate step in the direction he is about to throw the ball. This rule applies to a throw to any base or a pitch to the plate.

This balk rule prevents the pitcher from catching a base runner off guard by throwing too quickly and without warning. Without this rule it would be very easy for a pitcher to "pick a runner off" (catch the runner while he has stepped off his base).

This rule is often broken when the pitcher twirls towards a base and throws the ball in one fluid motion. The act of spinning or a quick pivot doesn't count as a deliberate step in the direction of the throw. Instead, he must spin, step, and throw.

6. Fake a throw to first base. The pitcher cannot fake a throw to first base or begin a throwing motion to first without completing the throw.

It's okay to fake a throw to second or third base as long as a runner is occupying the base, or the pitcher is making a play on a runner who may be approaching that base.

Note: If the pitcher throws to an unoccupied base he can be charged with delaying the game.

7. Make a pitching motion without completing the pitch. From the set or windup position the pitcher cannot begin a motion to pitch without completing the pitch.

Example: If the pitcher moves his pivot foot backward in a line with home base, it will be considered a pitching motion. If he then decides to throw to third base, a balk will be called. This is because he began his pitching motion by stepping in line with home plate but did not complete the pitch.

Step ahead of and toward the throw.

Step first

then throw

The step must precede the throw (even if only by a split second,) and the step must be in the direction of the throw.

The Balk	Eleven Ways to Balk	continued

8. Fake a pitch. The pitcher cannot fake a pitch or make a motion that could deceive a runner or batter. This type of balk can be called whether or not the pitcher has possession of the ball and whether or not he is touching the rubber.

Example: If the pitcher steps on the rubber without having possession of the ball, the umpire should interpret this as an intent to deceive the batter and a balk should be charged.

9. Delay of game. A balk can be called if the umpire feels that a pitcher is intentionally delaying the game.

10. Catcher outside the catcher's box during an intentional walk. A balk is called if an intentional ball is pitched when the catcher is outside of the catcher's box.

11. Drop the ball. A balk will be called if the pitcher drops the ball while on the rubber. It will also be a balk if a pitched ball slips out of his hands and fails to cross a foul line.

Note: No member of the opposing team may cause a pitcher to balk. This includes a manager, player, substitute, coach, trainer, bat boy, etc. For example, if a bat boy yells "time out," causing the pitcher to stop his pitch, the bat boy will be removed and the balk will be nullified.

Note: If the batter steps out of the batter's box after the pitcher has started his windup, the pitcher will be allowed to stop his pitching motion. See page 89.

The Strike Zone

The strike zone is an area over home plate. The width and depth is that of home plate, and the top and bottom of the strike zone is determined by the height and stance of the batter. If a legal pitch passes through any point in the strike zone, it's called a strike. If a pitch which isn't swung on doesn't pass through any point in the strike zone, it's called a ball.

The strike zone is defined by both the batter and home plate

top of shoulder
midpoint
top of pants

back of knees

Note: For an extensive description of the strike zone, see page 84 in the Batting chapter.

Strikes and Balls

Overview: A pitched ball can result in a strike, a ball, a foul, or a hit. This page explains the rules that define whether a pitch, when not successfully hit, is declared a strike or a ball.

A strike is called when:

1. A pitch passes through the strike zone and....	the batter does not swing the bat.
	the ball touches the batter. (This is a not considered a "hit by pitch.")
2. A pitch does *not* pass through the strike zone and...	the ball touches the batter as he attempts to hit it. (This is a not considered a "hit by pitch.")
3. On any pitch (strike zone or not)....	the batter swings but misses.
	the batter bunts the ball into foul territory.
	the batter, with less than two strikes against him, hits the ball into foul territory.
	the batter, with less than two strikes against him, hits a foul tip. (A "foul tip" occurs when the batter swings, the bat grazes the ball, and the ball goes directly into the catcher's mitt.)

A ball is called when:

1. A pitch does *NOT* pass through the strike zone and...	the batter does not swing.
2. A ball can also be called as a penalty against the pitcher for four infractions:	the pitcher makes an illegal pitch (such as a quick pitch) when no runners are on base.
	the pitcher delays the game when, with no runners on base, he does not pitch within twenty seconds of receiving the ball. (With runners on base, this delay will result in a balk.)
	the pitcher touches his pitching hand to his mouth while on the pitcher's mound.
	the pitcher (or an unidentified player on his team) defaces or otherwise tampers with the ball. (On the second offense, the pitcher will be ejected.)

Wild Pitches and Throws by the Pitcher

Overview: Wild pitches and wild throws are those that are unable to be caught by the catcher or a fielder "with ordinary effort" because the ball is thrown too high, too low, or too wide.

The rules governing wild pitches vary depending on where the ball ends up and whether the wild pitch occurred on the third strike or fourth ball. Similarly, wild throws by the pitcher are throws to a fielder unable to be caught with ordinary effort. They can end up in the dugout, stands, or otherwise go out of play.

On a wild pitch:

	the ball...	runners advance...
if the ball gets past the catcher but remains in fair territory....	remains in play	at own risk
if the pitch goes into an area where the ball is dead including the dugout, stands, and other areas that would make the ball unplayable....	is dead	1 base
if the ball deflects off the catcher into an area where the ball is dead....	is dead	1 base
if a pitch hits a runner attempting to score at home....	is dead	1 base
if a pitch (not the result of a foul tip) lodges in the umpire's or catcher's mask or equipment....	is dead	1 base

On a wild throw by the pitcher:

	the ball...	runners advance...
if a ball is thrown by the pitcher from his position on the plate to a fielder, and the ball goes into an area where it is dead....	is dead	1 base
if the pitcher steps off of the pitcher's rubber before making a wild throw, he is acting as an infielder. The wild throw rule for infielders applies....	is dead	2 bases

The third strike rule

When the catcher does not catch a pitch on the third strike and no one is on first base, or there's a runner on first with two outs, the batter is not out and must attempt to run to first base before being tagged out.

When a wild pitch occurs on a third strike, and results in any of the situations described in the above chart, the batter-runner is governed by the same rules as the other runners. He is awarded the same number of bases.

Example: If on a third strike a pitch gets past the catcher and becomes lodged in the umpire's mask, the batter advances to first base and all runners advance one base. See page 87 for more on the third-strike rule.

A batter hit by a wild pitch

A batter hit by a pitch is awarded first base. The ball is dead and runners advance only if they are forced to advance as a result of the batter going to first. (Also see Hit by a Pitch on page 94.)

Miscellaneous Pitching Rules

Taking hand signs

The official rulebook states that pitchers "must take signs from the catcher while standing on the rubber." While in this position, he may actually take signs from any member of his team, although typically signs come from the catcher.

Penalty. Accepting hand signs when not standing on the pitcher's rubber will result in a warning from the umpire (it is not a balk). However, with repeated offenses, the umpire may choose to eject the pitcher from the game.

Note: After receiving his signs a pitcher may elect to disengage the pitcher's rubber (step off the plate) or continue with the pitching sequence.

The pitcher becomes an infielder when he steps off the rubber

A pitcher becomes an infielder if he disengages the rubber by stepping off with his pivot foot. When he is off of the rubber, the pitcher may throw to any other base just like any other infielder. In this situation a wild throw by the pitcher is treated like a wild throw by an infielder. That is, the batter and runners may be awarded two bases on a wild throw that goes out of play (as opposed to one base if the wild throw occurred while he was throwing from his pitching position).

Attempting to hit the batter with a pitch

The pitcher, and possibly the manager and the pitcher, may be ejected from the game if, in the umpire's judgment, the pitcher pitches with the intention of hitting the batter. The umpire has the option, on the first offense, to issue a warning. Alternatively both teams may officially receive this warning from the umpire before the start of the game.

Because throwing with the intention of hitting the batter is dangerous behavior, in addition to being ejected from the game, a league president may take further action to punish the offenders.

Pitcher's uniform and glove

The rules impose special restrictions on the pitcher's uniform to minimize visual distractions.

• No numbers, letters, or insignias on the sleeve of his undershirt.

• The pitcher's glove cannot be white or gray, since those colors can obscure the ball. All parts of the glove — the stitching, lacing, and web — must be uniform in color, and no other material with a varying color can be attached to the glove.

As with other players, but especially the pitcher, glass buttons and any kind of shiny metal jewelry are not permitted.

A pitcher can be ejected from the game for the following:

• Having a foreign substance in his possession.

• Pitching with a tampered ball.

• Intentionally delaying the game by throwing the ball needlessly to other fielders when a batter is in position.

• Throwing the ball with the intention of hitting the batter.

• Continuing to take signs while not in his position on the pitcher's plate.

Ball Tampering: Spit Balls and More

Overview: Tampering with the ball is the act of wetting it, rubbing it with dirt or another foreign substance, discoloring it, or scuffing it, for the purpose of making it more difficult to hit. Simply put, the pitcher is not allowed to tamper with the ball in any way. If tampering is suspected, the umpire can demand to inspect the ball. He becomes the sole judge of whether a violation has occurred.

Intent of the rule. Tampering with the ball can affect the way the ball is thrown, its flight pattern, or otherwise make a pitched ball more difficult to hit. Ball tampering is therefore illegal.

Tampering	Types of Ball Tampering

A scuff can affect the flight of the ball by several inches .

Penalty. The penalty against the pitcher for either tampering with the ball or carrying an illegal substance will be:

- immediate ejection from the game, and
- an automatic ten day suspension.

Note 1: If a play continues after the violation is called, the offensive team's manager can elect to accept the play. He must notify the plate umpire immediately after the play is completed.

Illegal actions

The pitcher may not:

1. apply any "foreign substance" to the ball.

2. spit on the ball, his hand, or his glove.

3. rub the ball using his glove, body, or clothing (although he can rub the ball using his bare hands).

4. deface the ball in any way.

5. scuff the ball, or use what the official rule book terms the "emery ball."

6. touch his hand to his mouth (unless authorized by the umpire).

Illegal substances

The Official Rules of Major League Baseball bans specific substances from being carried onto the field. These include soil, rosin, paraffin, sandpaper, or emery paper. The rules go on, however, to cover themselves by adding any "other foreign substance" to the list of banned materials.

Illegal candy

There is a somewhat dated mention in the rules of the use of licorice as an illegal substance. It was used, at times, to discolor or mark the ball.

Note 2: In the case that the batter successfully reaches first base, and no other runner is put out, the play will count as if the violation had not occurred. This is the case regardless of whether the batter reached first base on a hit, an error, a walk, a hit batter, or other means.

Even with these exceptions, the tampering violation will be charged against the pitcher.

Note 3: If a player other than the pitcher is identified as the offender, that player will be immediately ejected from the game. However, if the pitcher pitches a ball that has been discolored or damaged and the umpire cannot identify the offender, the pitcher will be considered at fault.

Spit balls. A spit ball is a ball thrown after wetting the ball or the pitcher's fingers, using spit, sweat, Vaseline, or any other form of lubricant. Wetting makes it easier to throw the ball with little or no spin. A non-spinning ball can curve or drop more readily and can therefore be more difficult for the batter to hit.

Scuffed ball. A scuff, scratch or tear on the ball will affect its flight, creating greater aerodynamic drag on one side of the ball than the other. The ball will curve towards the scuffed side of the ball. The affect on the flight path can be slight, but even a small deviation can make a big difference for the batter.

Marked ball. A ball that has been discolored is also illegal, since it can be visually distracting or more difficult for the batter to see.

Hand-to-mouth rule. The pitcher is not allowed to touch his mouth or lips with his pitching hand while standing within the eighteen-foot diameter pitcher's mound. This is a less serious form of tampering.

Exception 1: In cold weather, if agreed upon by both managers prior to the start of the game, the umpire may allow pitchers to blow on their hands to warm them.

Exception 2: In cases where the pitch is completed and the batter reaches first base without any other runner being put out, the play will automatically count as if the violation had not occurred.

Penalty: As penalty for touching his mouth or lips, a "ball" may be called. Further, the league president can impose a fine for a pitcher's repeated violations.

The rosin bag

Pitchers are allowed to use a bag of rosin to help them get a good grip on the ball. The umpire-in-chief is responsible for making sure no one tampers with the rosin bag. He supplies a single bag to be used by all pitchers during that game. The rosin bag is placed on the back of the pitcher's mound, but if it's raining, the umpire may ask the pitchers to put the bag in their hip pocket. The pitcher can apply the rosin to his bare hands. No player is allowed to apply rosin directly to the ball, a glove or any part of a player's uniform.

Pitcher Substitutions

The starting pitcher

Prior to the start of the game, the managers of each team are required to hand their batting order to the umpire-in-chief. The pitcher whose name appears on the batting order cannot be substituted until the first batter, or a substitute for that batter, either reaches first base or is put out. The only exception would be when a starting pitcher becomes injured or ill, and if, in the judgment of the umpire, he is no longer able to play.

Substitute pitchers

A substitute pitcher may replace the current pitcher at any point in the game (provided the current pitcher has pitched through at least one batter's turn at bat). The original pitcher will not be eligible to play once he is removed from the game. However, a pitcher can be switched to another position and return to the pitcher's position at a later time.

Changing positions

Upon being substituted, a pitcher may assume another playing position rather than be removed from the game. However, a pitcher can only change positions once per inning.

Substitute pitchers while a batter is still at bat

When a substitute pitcher replaces the current pitcher while a batter is still at bat, the substitute pitcher must pitch to that batter (or to a substitute for that batter) until the batter reaches first base or is put out, or until the inning is over. The only exception would be if the substitute pitcher becomes injured or ill, and if, in the judgment of the umpire, he is no longer able to play.

Improper substitutes for the pitcher

In the case of an improper substitution for the pitcher, the umpire shall require the proper pitcher to return to complete his turn at the pitcher's mound.

Even in situations where, by mistake, the umpire-in-chief announces the substitution of an improper pitcher, the mistake, if caught, should be corrected before the improper pitcher begins pitching.

However, any play that takes place while an improper pitcher is pitching will be legal and will stand. As soon as the improper pitcher delivers a pitch to the batter, or as soon as a runner is put out, the improper pitcher is no longer improper — he becomes the proper pitcher and continues his turn at the mound. At this point, the manager cannot remove that pitcher until the batter has completed his turn at bat, or until the end of the half-inning. The umpire is required to notify the manager of this ruling.

Pitchers are allowed up to eight warmup pitches

The pitcher, either at the start of each inning or when substituting for another pitcher, may throw up to eight warmup pitches to the catcher. The warmup pitches should not exceed one minute of time. The umpire-in-chief may extend this in possible "emergency" cases, when the pitcher has not had adequate time to warm up prior to being called to the pitching mound.

Note: In televised games, the period in between innings is determined by the time allotted for television commercials. The pitcher is generally allowed to use as much of this time for warm up pitches as he wants.

Visits to the Pitcher's Mound

Visits to the pitcher's mound by a coach or manager

Simply stated, the coach or manager may visit the pitcher just once per inning. "Visiting" the pitcher means entering the pitcher's mound.

A coach or manager is allowed more than one visit to the mound if he is visiting more than one pitcher in the same inning. For instance, if the coach visits the pitcher's mound to remove a pitcher, and the manager visits the new pitcher that same inning, that will be considered one visit to the new pitcher.

Where a pitcher is substituted during a batter's turn at bat, the coach or manager may not make a second visit to the pitcher's plate while that batter is still at bat, even though the visit is to the new pitcher.

The manager cannot use another player to communicate with the pitcher in order to avoid a second visit. For example, if the coach or manager visits the catcher, and before the next pitch or play takes place, the catcher visits the pitcher, it will be considered a visit by the manager.

Exceptions: The manager or coach may freely talk to the pitcher before the completion of his eighth warm-up throw, and before the pitcher's one-minute time limit for warming up, without this talk being charged as a visit. If the team at bat calls a time out, a manager may also talk with the pitcher without that talk being counted as one of the visits – as long as the visit ends with the time out.

A second visit to a pitcher's mound

If a coach or manager visits the same pitcher for a second time in the same inning, that pitcher must be removed from the game, and a substitute pitcher must be named. There is no exception to this rule, even in the case when a pinch hitter has been substituted for a batter.

Penalty. If the manager persists in attempting to abuse this rule after being warned by the umpire, the manager will be immediately removed from the game. The pitcher will also be removed, at the conclusion of the current batter's turn at bat.

When this is the case the umpire should notify the manager that the pitcher is about to be removed from the game, so that a substitute pitcher can begin his warmup. If the umpire feels it is justified, the new pitcher may be allowed to take more than the usual eight warmup pitches when starting his turn at the mound.

A new pitcher resuming a suspended game

If a substitute pitcher is announced just before the call of a suspended game, the pitcher is not required to (but may) start the game when it is resumed. This is the case even when the pitcher did not complete the inning, or the batter to which he pitched did not complete a full turn at bat (as would be normally required). If he does not start pitching in the resumed game, however, he will be considered as being substituted and will not be allowed to play in the remainder of that game.

7 | Batting

Every offensive effort starts with a batter. It's where all the action begins in the game of baseball.

This chapter covers the rules concerning the batter, from the time he steps up to the plate, to the point when his turn at bat ends — either because he is out or because he became a runner. Included is a detailed description of the strike zone, the batter's box, and a list of every way a batter can get on base or be put out.

Batting: contents

Basics for the Batter

Overview: In order to understand many of the rules about batting, it will help to understand some terms and facts about the field. Here are a few basics.

| Basics | Key Areas of the Field |

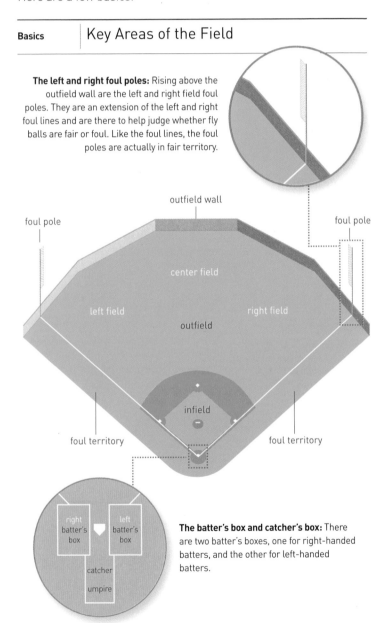

The left and right foul poles: Rising above the outfield wall are the left and right field foul poles. They are an extension of the left and right foul lines and are there to help judge whether fly balls are fair or foul. Like the foul lines, the foul poles are actually in fair territory.

outfield wall

foul pole

foul pole

center field

left field

right field

outfield

infield

foul territory

foul territory

right batter's box

left batter's box

catcher

umpire

The batter's box and catcher's box: There are two batter's boxes, one for right-handed batters, and the other for left-handed batters.

| Basics | Batting |

At the end of a player's turn at bat, one of two things will happen:

1. The batter gets on base. See page 92 for all the ways a batter can get on base.

2. The batter is out. See page 95 for all the ways a batter can be out.

If another player is put out to end the inning

If a runner is put out for the third out before the batter ends his turn at bat, then the batter will be the first batter up for his team in the next inning. His new turn at bat will start a new count of balls and strikes.

Every legal pitch will result in a ball, a strike, a foul, or a hit.

A batter is out after receiving three strikes. See page 84 for information on strikes.

A batter walks after receiving four balls, freely advancing to first base (see page 83 for details about balls and walks.

Foul balls are strikes. A ball hit foul is counted as a strike against the batter unless the batter already has two strikes, in which case the foul is ignored. The batter continues with the same count of strikes and balls.

Like a fair ball, however, a foul fly ball can be caught by a fielder for an out.

See pages 82 and 83 for more information about fair and foul balls.

| Basics | Bunting |

A bunt is a type of hit designed to deaden the ball so it will slowly roll into the infield. While some batters attempt to bunt for a base hit, typically the intent is to sacrifice the batter so that a runner will be able to advance to the next base.

When a batter bunts, he hits the ball without swinging the bat. Instead he holds the bat stationary and lets the ball bounce off the bat. The official rules, however, have no guidelines about what constitutes a bunt.

Bunting foul with two strikes is a strike — and an out.

The batter will be charged with a strike if he bunts the ball foul with two strikes against him. This will give him three strikes, and he will be out.

This is only true when bunting. Normally, if a batter fouls with two strikes, it is not counted as a strike. Because of this rule, it is rare to see a batter attempt a bunt once he has two strikes.

Basics	# Fair Balls

A fair ball is a ball hit into fair territory that is caught before it touches the ground, or that touches the ground and does not roll or bounce into foul territory before passing first or third base. If the ball bounces or rolls into foul territory after passing first or third base, it is still a fair ball.

If a fair ball touches the ground without being caught, the batter becomes a batter-runner and must run to first base. All other base runners may advance at risk of being tagged or thrown out.

If a fair ball is caught before touching the ground, the batter is out. Other base runners may only advance if they tag their current bases after the ball has been caught (see "Tagging Up" on page 112 in the Running chapter).

Examples: **Fair balls**

1. If a batted ball hits first or third base, it's considered a fair ball even if it then bounces into foul territory.

2. If a batted ball hits the foul line, it is considered a fair ball — unless it goes into foul territory before passing first or third base.

3. When a fly ball hits the foul pole it will be called a fair ball (and therefore a home run).

4. If a batted ball lands in foul territory and then rolls fair before passing first or third base, it is a fair ball.

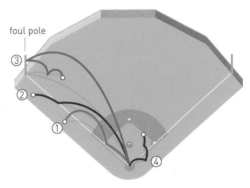

Examples: **Fair balls landing near home plate**

1. Home plate is in fair territory. If a batted ball bounces on home plate, it is a fair ball.

2. The foul lines extend through the batter's box, even though the white chalk lines are not drawn there. If a hit ball bounces within the batter's box, but inside the imaginary foul lines, it will be a fair ball

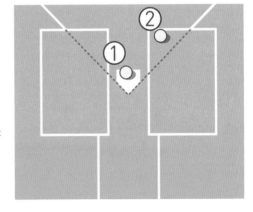

Basics | Foul Balls

A hit ball is foul when (1) it lands outside the foul lines in foul territory, or (2) it rolls or bounces into foul territory before passing first or third base.

- When a ball is hit foul the ball is dead. Runners may not advance or steal a base on a foul ball.

- If a ball hit into foul territory is caught before touching the ground, the batter is out, but the ball is still live. Runners will be allowed to tag up and advance (see Tagging Up on page 112 in the Running chapter).

- A foul is counted as a strike against the batter. However, a foul cannot result in a third strike. If the batter has two strikes against him, any foul balls he hits will simply be called dead — the count will remain at two strikes.

  Exception: If, with two strikes already in the count, a bunted ball goes foul, the batter will be out (see Bunting on page 81).

Examples: **Foul balls**

1. If a ball hits the ground in the infield and bounces or rolls into foul territory before going past first or third base, it is a foul.

2. If a fly ball lands outside of either foul line, whether in the stands or in foul territory, it is a foul.

3. If a fly ball goes over the outfield wall to the outside of either foul pole, it is a foul.

Basics | Balls and Walks (Base-On-Balls)

A *ball* is a pitch outside of the strike zone on which the batter does not swing. Once a batter receives four balls, he is awarded first base. This is called a "walk" or a "base-on-balls."

- When a batter is walked, any other base runners that are forced to advance will also be allowed to advance.

- When a pitch is called as a ball, the ball is still in play and runners may attempt to steal a base. If a pitch is dropped by the catcher, runners may also try to advance at risk of being put out.

- After a fourth ball is called, the ball is still live. Runners can steal a base. Even the batter being walked can attempt to advance to second base, at risk of being put out.

Intentional walks

If a pitcher chooses to walk a batter intentionally (by throwing pitches far outside the strike zone — also called a "pitch out"), the batter must remain within the batter's box. He can swing at the pitch, but he is not allowed to step outside the batter's box in an attempt to hit the ball.

Strikes and the Strike Zone

Overview: Even the most indifferent spectator knows that it takes "three strikes and you're out." The concept of strikes and the strike zone is one of the most fundamental rules in baseball. This section will cover the complex (and somewhat ambiguous) rules regarding strikes.

Strikes | ## The Strike Zone

The strike zone defines whether a pitch is a ball or a strike. It is an area in space located above home plate. The size and location of the strike zone is determined by the width and depth of home plate, and by the height and stance of the batter. If a legal pitch passes through any part of the strike zone, it's called a strike. If a pitch on which the batter does not swing fails to pass through the strike zone, it's called a ball.

Note: It is widely accepted that the strike zone varies from one umpire to the next, and even from one pitcher to the next. For instance, if a pitcher is well known as a strike-out pitcher, he may get the benefit of more strike calls than a rookie throwing pitches in the same area.

Strikes | ## The Strike Zone Size and Location

For each batter the umpire must use his judgment to imagine the size and area the strike zone occupies in space. He does this by using visual reference points that define the boundaries of the strike zone, as specified in the official rules.

top of shoulder
midpoint
top of pants
back of knees

The width of the strike zone is determined by the width of home plate — it remains the same for every batter. The upper and lower boundaries however are determined by points on the batter's body. The lower boundary is at the back of the knees, where the knees bend (more or less at the center of the knee caps). The upper boundary is the halfway point between the waist and the shoulders (more or less at the letters spelling the team name on his chest).

The strike zone is a three dimensional area the exact shape of home plate. If a ball passes through any point in the three dimensional space, it will be called a strike.

| Strikes | ## The Strike Zone and a Batter's Stance |

The height of the strike zone depends on the stance of the batter during his normal swing. It becomes shorter if the batter crouches and taller if he is more upright.

Note: It doesn't matter how low the batter crouches as he is waiting for the pitch. The strike zone is determined during the batter's normal swing.

| Strikes | ## The Strike Zone and a Batter's Height |

On August 19, 1951, Eddie Gaedel, a midget, was put into the St. Louis Browns line up by manager Bill Veeck. At only three feet seven inches. Eddie Gaedel is an excellent example of how the strike zone is relative to a batter's height.

The strike zone for Eddie Gaedel was about a foot high — a difficult target for any pitcher. Gaedel was walked in his first and only at-bat.

To the right, Sammy Sosa and his strike zone is shown at the same scale as Eddie Gaedel's.

Rules vs. Reality

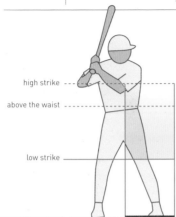

high strike

above the waist

low strike

The official strike zone

The rules say the strike zone should extend from the knees to the midpoint between the batter's waist and shoulders.

The strike zone in actual use

Although the strike zone varies according to the style and judgment of each umpire, few major league umpires will call a "high strike" (a pitch near the top of the legal strike zone). In fact, until recent years, umpires typically called the top of the strike zone just above the waist.

A tale of two strike zones

At one time, there was a difference between the strike zones called in the American League and the National League. This came about because of different chest protectors in use at the time. The American League umpires wore a bulky foam rubber "outside" chest protector (also called a "balloon protector") that prevented them from crouching very low. In the National league, the umpires wore a lighter "inside" chest protector that allowed them to crouch lower and call the lower end of the strike zone more accurately. As a result, the American League had a higher strike zone than the National League.

In the seventies, the American League adopted the inside protector. More recently, umpires from both leagues have joined to become a unified entity.

Now all umpires call pitches from a position known as "the slot." They crouch low and view the pitch between the catcher and batter, as shown in the diagram below.

the slot

This photo shows umpire Emmett Ashford wearing a balloon protector. He was the first black umpire to join professional baseball in 1954.

Strikes	The Third Strike Rule

As everyone knows, after three strikes, the batter is always out. Well, almost always. There is a loophole. In certain cases, whether the batter swings or not, if the catcher misses a catch on the third strike, the batter is not out and may attempt to run to first base.

This rule applies when:

1. there is no runner on first base, or

2. there is a runner on first and two outs.

Note: Even though it may seem to be a disadvantage for the batter that the third strike rule is not allowed if there is a runner on

first base with less than two outs, this condition is actually in the offensive team's best interest. It prevents the defensive team from making an easy double play. In most cases, a missed or dropped third strike is picked up quickly by the catcher, who either throws the batter out easily at first base, or is able to tag the batter before he is able to get far from the batter's box. If a runner on first was forced to run to second because of a missed or dropped third strike, it would typically end in a double play. The catcher throws to second for the first out, and the second baseman

throws to first base to make the second out.

If this condition were not in place, the catcher could be tempted to miss the catch intentionally and make an easy double play.

If the missed catch rolls out of play

If the batter swings and misses for his third strike, the catcher misses the catch, and the ball goes off the field and out of play (even if it bounced off the umpire), the batter will be awarded first base. Any base runners at the time of the play will also be awarded one base. The ball is dead.

Strikes	Check Swing: How Much Is Too Far?

If a batter stops the motion of his swing before pivoting too far, it will not count as a swing. This is called a "check swing" (or a "half-swing"), and the pitch will be called a strike or a ball according to the location of the pitch. This is a judgment call by the umpire. A check swing is not actually defined in the rules.

One indication of when a batter swings to far is if the head of his bat swings past the foul line or the front of home plate. Another indication is if the batter "breaks" his wrist, meaning he bends his wrist as he commits to the swing. (Also see page 143 in the Umpires chapter.)

Appealing the call

Often the defensive team will disagree with the home plate umpire's judgment concerning whether a batter went too far with his swing. The defensive team can make an appeal if they feel that a batter should be charged with a swing for a strike. If the batter is right handed, the catcher will appeal to the first base umpire. If the batter is left handed, the appeal will be made to the third base umpire. These umpires have the final word because they have the best view of whether the head of the bat passed the first or third base line. After the swing, the catcher can make the appeal by pointing at the appropriate umpire.

Example: One way to judge a check swing

Check swing: If the batter is able to stop the swing before the head of the bat crosses the foul line, it is not considered a full swing.

Full swing: If the head of the bat crosses the foul line, it is considered a full swing.

Illegal Bats

Overview: If a tampered bat is detected, the batter will be called out and ejected from the game. If the ball was hit, no runners will be allowed to advance, but any outs made on the play will stand.

18 inch handle area

One solid piece of wood

The bat must be carved from a solid piece of wood with no foreign materials added.

The handle

The handle area can be treated with any substance or material to improve the grip, but it must not extend more than eighteen inches from the bottom. Typically, pine tar is used for this purpose, and applied to the bat with a rag.

Too much pine tar

If a bat is discovered to have pine tar above eighteen inches, it will be removed from the game without penalty to the batter. If the bat has already been used in the game, it will not be grounds for ejecting or even calling the batter out.

See page 39 for complete bat specifications.

Tampering with a bat

There are several ways a batter might try to gain an advantage by modifying his bat. Perhaps the best known is corking, but the rules also mention bats that are filled, flattened, nailed, hollowed, grooved, or covered with wax.

How to cork a bat

It's a fairly simple process, and most any ball player could manage it if properly motivated.

A hole about one inch in diameter is drilled into the bat and filled with pieces of cork, rubber, or any light material. The hole is then plugged with wood filler so no one is the wiser — until the bat breaks.

Cork

The great corked-bat caper

In 1994 a corked bat belonging to Albert Belle was confiscated by the umpire. During the game, Jason Grimsley, Belle's teammate, crawled through the ceiling into the umpire's locker room to replace the corked bat with a unaltered bat. All of Belle's bats were corked, so Grimsley (thinking fast) used another teammate's bat. Unfortunately, the switch was noticed immediately, in part because the replacement bat bore the name of the other player.

Calling Time Out

Overview: The batter cannot just step out of the batter's box at his own discretion. Once the pitcher is in position the batter must stay in position, or request a time out from the plate umpire.

Note: Umpires tend to discourage batters from taking too many time outs and slowing the game down. They will often make exceptions based on special circumstances, such as adverse weather conditions or a pitcher taking too much time.

When a time out is not allowed

The pitcher goes through several steps in the pitching sequence. Once he has left the set or windup step in the sequence, the batter will not be granted a time out for any reason — even if he claims he has something in his eye, he missed a sign, or he provides any other excuse. Remember that the pitcher's motion is quick between taking signs and moving into the set or windup position (see page 64 in the Pitching chapter for details on the pitching motion). In some cases the umpire may allow a time out right up to the instant the pitcher gets to the set or windup step in the sequence.

If the batter steps away with no time out

If the batter steps away from the batter's box without being granted a time out, the pitcher can throw a pitch and the umpire will rule it a strike or a ball accordingly.

If a pitch is thrown during a time out

If the pitcher throws a pitch after a time out has been granted, the ball is ruled dead and the pitch will not count.

If a batter refuses to take his position

If for any reason the batter refuses to take his place in the batter's box, the umpire will order the pitcher to pitch, and each pitch will be called a strike even if the pitch is outside the strike zone.

Note: With a runner on base, if the batter steps out of the box after the pitcher has started his windup, the pitcher will be allowed to stop his pitching motion without throwing the ball. A balk will not be called against him. See "The Balk" on page 68.

When is it too late for a batter to call time out?

Too late to call time out

 |

While the pitcher is taking signs, and until the point that the pitcher commits to the pitch, the batter will usually be allowed to call time out.

After the pitcher leaves the set or windup position, the batter will not be granted a time out.

The Batter's Box

Overview: The batter's box is an area next to home plate indicated by white chalk lines. The batter must stand in the box when batting. Rules concerning the exact position of his feet within the box depend on whether the batter is waiting for the pitch, swinging the bat, or running after hitting the ball.

The batter's box

The batter's box is actually two identical boxes on each side of home plate. One box is for right-handed batters and the other is for left-handers.

Dimensions

At four by six feet, the box is big enough for a full swinging movement by the batter. The area behind the box designated for the catcher and umpire is far enough away from the batter to avoid hitting the catcher during the swing.

Note: The box is actually defined by the outer edges of the white chalk lines. In some ballparks the lines nearest to home plate are not drawn.

Batter's Box | # Waiting, Swinging, and Running

There are three basic stages of batting: waiting for the pitch, swinging the bat at the ball, and running once the ball has been hit. For each of these stages there are specific rules that dictate where the batter's feet should be positioned within the batter's box.

Waiting for the pitch

Legal: His foot is on the line but not across the line.

Illegal: His foot is crossing the outer edge of the line.

Before the pitch is thrown, the batter must stand completely within the box. His feet may touch the white chalk line but should never cross the outer edge of the line.

Penalty: The batter may be warned to change to a legal position. If the batter makes contact with the ball while in an illegal position, he will be out.

Swinging the bat at the ball

Legal: At least some portion of his foot is still within the box or touching the line.

Illegal: His foot is completely past the outer edge of the line and therefore out of the box.

The batter may step partly across the outer edge of the line while making contact with the ball during his swing, but his foot must be touching the line. He must never step completely outside of the line.

Penalty: If he makes contact with the ball while one foot is completely outside of the box, the batter is out and the ball is dead.

Running: touched by a hit ball

Foul: If a hit ball touches the batter when he has at least one foot still on the ground inside the box, the hit is called a foul, and the ball is dead.

Out: If a hit ball touches the batter when both feet are outside the box, or if one foot is in the air and the other is outside the box, the batter is out and the ball is dead.

If a hit ball comes into contact with the batter as he leaves the batter's box, the umpire's call will depend on the position of the batter's feet when the contact was made.

Getting on Base

Overview: A batter can reach a base either by becoming a runner (at the risk of being put out) or by being awarded bases. There are two ways he can be allowed to run. There are eighteen ways he can be awarded bases.

On Base	Ways a Batter Becomes a Runner

1. The batter hits the ball into fair territory. If a hit ball touches the ground in fair territory before being caught by a fielder, the batter becomes a runner and must run to first base.

2. The catcher drops or misses a third strike. Under certain conditions, if the catcher misses the pitch on a third strike, on a pitch where the batter made no contact with the ball, the batter becomes a runner and may run to first base (see page 87).

On Base	Ways a Batter Can be Awarded First Base

1. The pitcher has thrown four balls. Once the pitcher throws four balls, the batter is entitled to a *walk* (also called a "base-on-balls"). He will be allowed to advance to first base without risk.

2. The batter is hit by a pitch. When a batter is hit by a pitch he will be awarded first base. The ball will be dead and other runners will not be allowed to advance (unless forced) — even if the ball deflects off the batter in such a way that the catcher is unable to catch the ball.

Important: There are three conditions for awarding first base under this rule:

a. The pitch must not be in the strike zone.

b. The batter must not be swinging at the ball.

c. The batter must attempt to get out of the way.

See page 94 for more about being hit by a pitch.

3. The catcher interferes with the batter. If a catcher interferes with a batter while he is trying to hit a pitch, the batter will be awarded first base.

4. On the third strike, the pitch goes out of play. If on a third strike, the ball is not caught by the catcher and gets stuck in the catcher's or umpire's mask, or it rolls or is deflected into the dugout or off the field, the batter will be allowed to advance to first base.

5. An umpire or a runner is touched by a hit ball. The batter will be awarded first base if a fair batted ball touches an umpire before it touches a fielder. The same is true if the ball touches a runner before it touches a fielder — but in this case, while the batter is awarded first, the runner will be called out.

Note: If an umpire or runner is touched by the ball after it has been in contact with a fielder, the ball simply remains in play.

6. A fielder obstructs the batter-runner. If not in possession of the ball, a fielder may not obstruct a batter-runner (or any other runner) or cause him to miss touching his base. If this occurs the fielder will be charged with obstruction and the batter-runner (or the affected runner) will be considered to have reached the base.

On Base | # Ways a Batter Can be Awarded Second Base

---

7. Fielder throws his glove to stop a thrown ball. If a fielder intentionally throws his glove, cap or any piece of equipment at a *thrown* ball, and hits the ball, the ball is dead. The batter and all runners are awarded two bases.

8. Fielder uses his cap to catch a thrown ball. If a fielder uses his cap, uniform or anything but his hand or glove to catch a *thrown* ball, and touches the ball, the ball is dead and all runners are awarded two bases.

On Base | # Awarded Second Base: Ground Rule Doubles

If a fair ball bounces or rolls completely out of play, the umpire will rule the ball dead, and all base runners (including the batter) will be awarded two bases. This rule is in the best interest of the defense because it puts a limit on the number of bases a runner can advance.

Examples: Ground rule doubles

9. A fair ball bounces over the outfield wall.

10. A fair ball bounces out of play and goes into the stands, the dugout or anywhere out of play.

11. A fair ball gets stuck somewhere or goes through or under a wall, lodges in a fence or vines.

12. A fair ball is deflected. After touching the ground, a fielder deflects the ball over the outfield wall or any other area where it is out of play.

13. A fair ball is kicked or deflected into the stands or dugout. This is a ground rule double whether or not the ball touched the ground first.

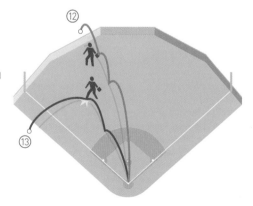

Note: If a ballpark has an outfield wall in fair territory that is shorter than 250 feet from home plate, any hit ball that flies, bounces, or is deflected over it will be a ground rule double and not a home run.

| **On Base** | Ways a Batter Can be Awarded Third Base |

14. Fielder throws his glove to stop a batted ball. If a fielder throws his glove, cap or any piece of equipment at a *batted* ball, and it touches the ball, the ball is dead and all runners (including a batter runner) are awarded three bases.

15. Fielder tries to catch a batted ball with his cap. If a fielder tries to catch a *batted* ball with his cap, shirt, or anything but his hand or glove, the batter and all other runners will be awarded three bases at the end of playing action.

Note: Even though these last two points seem like bad behavior on the part of the fielder, there is no consequence whatsoever — including no awarded bases — if the ball is not touched.

| **On Base** | Ways a Batter Can be Awarded a Home Run |

16. Batter hits a home run. A ball that is hit over the outfield fence, between the left and right foul poles, earns the batter a home run. If the ball hits either of the foul poles, it is still considered fair and will qualify as a home run.

17. Deflected home run. If, without touching the ground, a fair ball bounces off a player and over the outfield fence, it will be a home run.

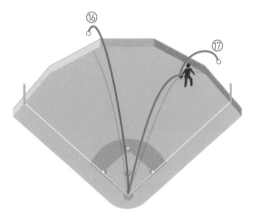

Hit by a Pitch

When a batter is hit by a pitch he will be awarded first base. The ball will be dead and no other runners will be allowed to advance (unless forced) — even if the ball deflects off the batter in such a way that the catcher is unable to catch the ball.

Important: There are three conditions for awarding first base under this rule:

a. The pitch must not be in the strike zone. When a pitch is in the strike zone it's the batter's responsibility to get out of the way of the ball. When a batter is hit by a strike, there will be no bases awarded and the pitch will be called a strike.

b. The batter must not be swinging at the ball. If the batter was hit while he was swinging at the pitch, there will be no bases awarded. The pitch will be called a strike, the same as if the batter swung without making contact with the ball.

c. The batter must attempt to get out of the way. If in the judgment of the umpire, a batter made no attempt to dodge the oncoming pitch, there will be no bases awarded. The pitch will simply be called a strike or ball, as appropriate.

Making an Out

Overview: At the end of every at-bat, one of two things will happen — the batter will safely reach a base, or he will be out. The following is a list of all the ways a batter can be called out.

Making an Out	Sixteen Ways a Batter is Out

1. A fly ball is caught. The hit must be caught, in either fair or foul territory, before it touches the ground.

2. Three strikes. The batter is out as soon as he receives his third strike (unless the third strike is dropped by the catcher — page 87).

3. First base is tagged. When the batter hits the ball he is forced to run to first base. A fielder in possession of the ball can tag first base before the batter reaches it for an out.

4. The batter is tagged. After hitting the ball, the batter-runner is out if tagged by a fielder in possession of the ball before the batter-runner is able to reach his base.

5. Bunts foul with two strikes. With two strikes in the count, a bunted ball that goes foul is counted as a third strike, putting the batter out (page 81).

6. The infield fly rule is called. The infield fly rule results in an automatic out for the batter while the hit is still in the air. This call averts a possible double play (page 131).

7. A fielder intentionally drops a fly ball. If an umpire believes that a fielder intentionally dropped an infield fly (likely in an attempt to make a double play), the umpire will call the batter out and the ball dead (page 131).

8. A hit touches the batter. If a fair ball touches the batter before touching a fielder, the batter will be called out.

9. The batter alters the path of a hit ball. If the batter intentionally interferes with a hit ball in a way that alters its path, for instance, by throwing his helmet at it, he's out.

10. The bat hits the ball twice. If the batter somehow manages to hit a pitched ball twice, he will be called out.

11. The batter runs outside the base paths. When more than halfway to first base and with the fielders attempting to make a play at first base, the batter must not step to the left of the foul line and must stay within a three-foot distance from the right of the foul line, unless he is trying to avoid interfering with a fielder or the play (pages 96 and 114).

12. Batter steps outside of the batter's box. If the batter hits the ball while one or both feet are outside the batter's box, he will be out (page 91).

13. Batter switches between the right and left batter's box. If the batter switches from one side of home plate to the other while the pitcher is in pitching position, he will be called out (page 173).

14. Batter interferes with the catcher. If the batter steps out of the batter's box to intentionally interfere with the catcher, he will be called out (page 96).

15. The batter is caught with a tampered bat. If the umpire believes the batter is using an illegal bat, he will call the batter out. (page 88).

Out as a result of a teammate's action.

16. A runner interferes with a fielder. If a runner intentionally interferes with a fielder trying to make a double play, the batter will be called out — even though he wasn't involved in the interference (See "Interference by a Runner" on page 119).

Offensive Interference by the Batter

Overview: Offensive interference is an act by a batter or runner to disrupt a fielder making a play. In many cases the umpire must believe the act to be intentional in order to make the call.

Interference	Types of Interference by a Batter

Interfering with the catcher

The batter will be called out for interference if he steps outside of the batter's box to intentionally interfere with the catcher receiving or throwing the ball. That is not to say that it's okay to interfere while inside the box, but because of the distance between the batter and catcher, if the batter was able to interfere with the catcher while still in the batter's box, the catcher would be too close to home plate.

Example: It is interference if the batter blocks the catcher's attempt to throw to a base when trying to put out a runner stealing a base.

The batter also cannot interfere with a catcher's return throw to the pitcher, or try to prevent a catcher from catching a pop foul.

Penalty: On the call of interference, the batter is out and the ball is dead. No runners will be allowed to advance — they must return to the bases they last legally occupied.

Hitting the catcher during the swing

It is not considered interference if the batter, when swinging his bat, swings completely around and unintentionally hits or hinders the catcher. As long as the batter remained within the batter's box, the pitch will simply be called a strike (even if the bat came completely around and hit the ball on the back swing).

However, if the bat does hit the catcher, unlike a typical strike, the ball will be dead and base runners will return to the bases they last legally occupied.

This prevents the batter from interfering with the catcher to help a runner. Because the ball will be dead, a runner attempting to steal a base during this play will be unable to benefit from the batter's actions — he must return.

Throwing the bat or equipment

If, when swinging, the entire (unbroken) bat slips and flies into fair territory, hitting or otherwise interfering with a fielder, interference will be charged against the batter.

The batter will also be charged with interference if he throws his helmet or any other object into the path of a hit or thrown ball (whether he hits it or not), or toward a fielder with the intention of interfering with a play.

If the bat breaks and a piece of the bat hits the ball or a fielder, the batter will not be charged with interference. Since this happened unintentionally, the ball remains in play.

Running outside the base path

If the ball is being fielded at first base following a hit, once the batter has run more than half the distance between home and first base he may not step to the left of the foul line or step more than three feet to the right of the foul line. Stepping on the foul line is okay.

If the umpire believes the batter has stepped beyond these boundaries and in so doing interfered with a fielder making a play, the batter will be called out for interference.

Exception: The batter is required to step outside these boundaries if he needs to avoid interfering with the fielder's play.

Interference	By a Batter and a Runner

If a runner is put out on the play

If the batter interferes with the catcher (or any other fielder) making a play, but a runner is put out on the play despite the batter's actions, then interference will not be called and the batter will not be out.

Example 1: A runner attempts to steal second base. The batter interferes with the catcher while he is trying to make a throw to put the runner out. If the catcher successfully makes the throw and the runner is put out, interference will not be called.

Example 2: A batter-runner interferes with the first baseman by running into him after stepping on first base. The first baseman is able to throw out a runner attempting to run home despite the batter's actions. Interference is not called.

The batter and the runner can be called out due to interference by the runner.

If, after a hit, a runner already on base intentionally interferes with a fielder trying to make a play on a hit or thrown ball, both the batter and the runner will be called out.

If there are two outs, the batter (not the runner) will be the player called out.

This harsh two-out penalty was put in place to discourage unsportsmanlike conduct, whereby a runner could deviate from his running path to intentionally interfere with a fielder making a play.

Example: During a possible double play, a runner from first base will often try to slide into the second baseman to prevent him from successfully throwing the ball to first base in time to throw the batter out.

Typically, runners are given some leeway in this particular example. The act would have to be flagrant for the umpire to call interference.

Defensive Interference Against the Batter

Interference by the catcher against the batter.

If a catcher (or any other fielder) is judged by the umpire to have hindered the batter in any way during his swing, the catcher or fielder will be charged with interference.

Penalty: The batter will be awarded first base. The ball is dead and base runners who are forced to advance will be allowed to advance.

Note 1: The manager of the offensive team may decide to reject the call of interference if he feels it is to his team's advantage. It becomes his choice whether to accept the awarded bases or accept the results of the completed play.

Example: With a runner on third base and one out, the batter gets a hit, but the catcher interfered with the batter during the swing. The batter is thrown out at first, but the runner from third scores at home. The manager may accept the interference penalty which puts the batter on first base but requires the runner to remain on third base. Or he may choose to reject the call of interference, in which case the batter will be out but the runner on third will have scored a run.

Note 2: In cases in which defensive interference occurs but the batter successfully reaches first base and all the other runners successfully advance at least one base, the interference will be automatically ignored, since it will be judged to have had no effect.

The Batting Order

Overview: The manager of each team determines the sequence in which his nine players will come to bat. This is called the "batting order" (also referred to as "the lineup"). This section discusses the batting order and what happens if a batter bats out of turn.

Batting Order	Presenting the Batting Order

The batting order is determined before the start of the game.

Players must come to bat in the sequence specified in the team's batting order. Five minutes prior to the start of the game, the manager of the home team hands two identical copies of the batting order to the umpire-in-chief. Next, the manager of the visiting team does the same. The umpire-in-chief checks to make sure each of the duplicates are, in fact, identical. He then gives each manager a copy of the opposing teams batting order, keeping one copy of each for himself.

At this point the batting order becomes official and the sequence cannot be altered.

Starting the game. The visiting team will be the first team at bat, and the first player on the visiting team's batting order takes his place in the batter's box. With this action, the umpire calls "play" and the game begins.

Likewise, the first player on the home team's batting order shall be the first batter for that team.

At the beginning of each subsequent inning, the starting batter is the player whose name appears after the player who last completed his turn at bat in the previous inning.

Substitutions. If during the game, a substitute player takes the place of a player, the substitute must bat in that player's position in the batting order.

Errors in the batting order should be corrected immediately.

Teams are not liable for obvious errors in the batting orders handed to the umpire. If a batting order contains fewer than nine names, or if two players with identical last names appear on the list and are not differentiated, the mistake should simply be corrected before the umpire calls "play." If these problems are discovered after the start of the game, they should be corrected at that time.

(See page 34 for additional details on presenting the batting order.)

Batting Order	Batting Out of Turn: Improper Batters

A batter who bats out of turn in the batting order is considered an "improper batter." The umpire, if he is the first to notice that a batter is out of order, shall not call this violation on his own. He must wait until the players or managers on either team take action.

The course of action taken depends on whether the violation is corrected by the batter's team, or if and when it is called to the attention of the umpire in an appeal by the defensive team.

| Batting Order | Three Ways to Deal with an Improper Batter |

There are three basic circumstances in which an improper batter may be handled. The actions taken depend on when the improper batter is called to the attention of the umpire. The umpire can be notified by the offensive team, or by the defensive team in an appeal:

1. before the end of the improper batter's turn at bat.

2. after the improper batter completes his turn at bat.

3. after a pitch has been thrown to the next batter or any other play has been made.

The repercussions of each are explained below.

1. Before the end of the improper batter's turn at bat

There is no penalty if the defensive team makes an appeal or if the offensive team corrects their mistake while the improper batter is still at bat. The proper batter simply switches places with the improper batter. Play will continue exactly where it left off, and any strikes and balls incurred by the improper batter will be applied toward the proper batter's count.

2. After the improper batter completes his turn at bat

The defensive team can make an appeal after the improper batter completes his turn at bat, but must do so before another play is attempted or before a pitch is made to the next batter. On the appeal, the batter who missed his turn at bat (not the improper batter) will be declared out for violating the batting sequence. Any plays or advances made as the result of the improper batter's performance will be nullified. Outs, if any, will not count and all runners will return to their positions as if the improper batter had not come to bat. The proper batter will come to the plate (even if that means that the previously improper batter must bat again).

Any advances or plays that were not the result of the improper batter's turn at bat, such as runners advancing due to a stolen base, a balk or a wild pitch, will stand. See the examples on the following page.

3. After a pitch has been thrown to the next batter, or after any other play has been made

If the defensive team appeals to the umpire about the batting-out-of-turn violation after a pitch or play has been made, it is too late for any action to be taken. Once a play takes place, the "improper batter" has become the "proper batter" and the game continues as if no mistake had been made. Anything that occurred as a result of the improper batter's turn at bat (hits, outs, runs, etc.) is now considered legal.

Since the improper batter's turn at bat is now considered legal, the batting order jumps to the batter following the improper batter in the lineup. In other words, the next proper batter is the person whose name appears on the batting order following the out-of-turn batter's name. Any batter who was skipped simply misses his turn at bat.

| Improper Batter Examples

Example 1: Improper batter

Batter 1 is due up next
in the batting order, but
batter 2 bats in his place
and hits a double.

Batter 3 comes to the
plate and waits for the first
pitch.

If the appeal is made....

1. Before the next pitch or play:

- batter 1 is called out because he was
  the batter who missed his turn.

- batter 2's hit doesn't count.

- batter 2 is the next batter because he
  comes after the last proper batter on
  record.

2. After the next pitch is made to batter 3, or after a play is attempted:

- batter 3 is now the proper batter
  because as soon as the next pitch
  or play was made batter 2 became a
  proper batter. Batter 1 missed his turn.

- batter 2 stays on second.

Example 2: Improper batter

With batter 1 on third base
and batter 3 on first, batter
5 bats out of turn.

On a wild pitch with batter
5 at bat, batter 1 scores
from third while batter 3
advances to second.

Batter 5 grounds out,
sending batter 3 to third.

If the appeal is made....

1. Before the next pitch or play:

- batter 1's run and batter 3's advance
  to second count, because they were
  the result of a defensive error (the wild
  pitch) rather than the actions of the
  improper batter.

- batter 3 goes back to second because
  his advance to third was the result of
  the improper batter's batting.

- batter 4 is called out for missing his
  turn at bat.

- batter 5 is now the proper batter,
  coming to the plate again to start a
  new at-bat.

2. After the next pitch is made to batter 3, or after a play is attempted:

- batter 1's run counts.

- batter 3 stays on third.

- batter 5 is considered a proper batter.

- batter 6 comes to bat.

A proper batter is already on base.

If things get really out of hand, it's conceivable that several improper batters could follow each other in succession. As a result, the next proper batter could even be on base at the time that an appeal is finally made. In this event, the batting order will skip to the next available batter.

The Designated Hitter

Overview: The designated hitter rule allows a player who has no fielding duties to bat in place of the pitcher. The rule has been adopted by the American League but not by the National League.

History

In 1973, the New York Yankees became the first team to use a designated hitter (often referred to as the "DH").

The rule was implemented to liven up the game and has been controversial since its inception. Opponents of the rule feel that it eliminates some of the strategic complexities that make the game so interesting. They suggest that fans who want to see aging sluggers get a few more runs for excitement should try another sport — like arena football.

American League managers are not required to use a designated hitter, but to do so they need to name him in the batting order at the start of the game.

The rule

The designated hitter bats in place of the starting pitcher and any substitute pitcher for his team throughout the game. He is not required to participate as a fielder.

The designated hitter named in the batting order must come to bat at least once in a game, unless the opposing team changes pitchers.

During the game, the manager can replace the designated hitter with a pinch hitter (the term for a substitute batter), but he must come to bat at least once in a game, unless the opposing team changes pitchers.

Once a designated hitter has been replaced by a substitute, he may not play in the game in any position. Similarly, if the designated hitter is replaced by a pinch runner, that new runner becomes the designated hitter.

The person identified as the designated hitter must always bat in the same place in the batting order. Multiple substitutions cannot be made that will alter the DH position in the batting order.

A designated hitter may take a fielding position during the game, replacing another fielder, but the pitcher must then bat in the replaced fielder's position in the batting order.

Pinch hitter

Although a designated hitter hits in place of the pitcher, he should not be confused with a substitute or a pinch hitter. He is part of the lineup from the start of the game. A pinch hitter is a substitute, replacing another player in his turn at bat. The player he replaces is considered substituted and is thus out of the game.

8 | Running

The goal of the runner is to advance around the bases until he reaches home plate to score a run for his team. It may sound simple, but many things can happen as he makes his way around the bases.

This chapter is about the rules concerning base running, including information about force plays, obstruction, missing a base, and other topics.

Running: contents

Basics for the Runner

Overview: A runner's objective is to get from one base to the next without being put out. Specifications for the base paths are shown below.

The base paths are six feet wide and each base is ninety feet apart. Just outside of first and third bases are the base coaches' boxes. The base coaches are allowed to signal advice to runners and batters as long as they don't interfere with the play.

Dimensions of the base paths

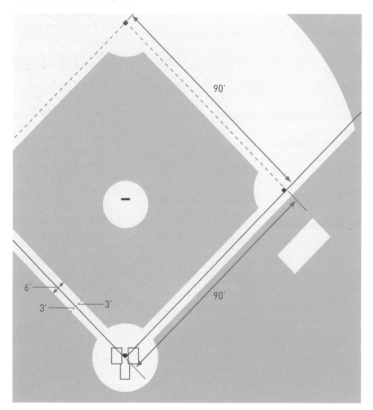

Note: The official rules refer to a batter on his way to first base as a "batter-runner." This somewhat awkward term is used in this chapter, and throughout the book, to distinguish a batter who has just become a runner from the other runners.

Twelve Ways a Runner Can Be Put Out

Overview: Once a batter has successfully reached a base, he becomes a runner. Here are twelve ways a runner can be put out.

1. **Tagged out by a fielder.** A runner can be tagged out by a fielder with the ball, provided the ball is in play and the runner is not touching his base.

2. **Fielder tags a base on a force play.** When a runner is forced to advance to a base, he can be put out without being tagged. Instead, a fielder with possession of the ball can simply tag the base he is running to. See "Force Plays" on page 106.

3. **Misses a base.** If a runner misses a base, and continues to advance to the next base, the defensive team can tag the runner or the base he missed. They can also appeal after the play is over.

4. **Fails to "tag up" before advancing after a fly ball is caught.** Runners are allowed to advance on a hit (fair or foul) that is caught for an out, but they must touch their base after the catch is made before attempting to advance. If they fail to do so, the defensive team can appeal once the play is over. The appeal is made by tagging the original base. The appeal must be made before another play takes place. See page 112.

5. **Runs outside the baseline.** If to avoid being tagged a runner runs more than three feet away from the baseline, he will be called out (unless he is trying to avoid interfering with a fielder making a play). See page 114.

6. **Passes another runner.** A runner is out if he passes a runner ahead of him on the bases.

7. **Touched by a batted ball.** A runner is out if a ball hit into fair territory touches him before it passes or is touched by a fielder. When this happens:

- the batter advances to first base,
- the ball is dead, and
- no other runners score or advance unless they are forced to advance.

See page 115.

Exception: Different rules apply if the hit is an infield fly. See page 131.

8. **Does not immediately return to first base.** Even though a runner is allowed to run or slide past first base, the runner must immediately return to first base or else he can be put out. See page 111, "Overrunning First Base."

9. **Abandons the bases.** If a runner leaves his base, abandoning his attempt to (eventually) reach subsequent bases, the umpire can rule him out.

This is not an appeal play. This situation may occur by mistake. For example, if a runner mistakenly believes he was put out, or thinks the half-inning is over, and he heads towards the dugout, by walking away from the base he can be called out. See page 111, "Abandoning the Bases."

10. **Interferes with a thrown ball or a fielder.** The runner must never intentionally interfere with a thrown ball or interfere with a fielder making a play on a ball. See "Interference by a Runner" on page 119 .

11. **Batter interferes.** A runner can be called out when a batter interferes with the play at home plate while a runner is attempting to score. See page 121.

12. **Runs the bases in reverse.** A runner will be called out if, after successfully reaching a base, he runs the bases in reverse order. This rather odd rule is intended to prevent the runner from intentionally tricking or distracting a fielder. This action must be intentional and does not apply to a runner who runs back to a previous base because he mistakenly believes a ball was caught or because he was deceived by a fielder.

Force Plays: When a Runner Is Forced to Advance

Overview: When a batter becomes a runner and attempts to reach first base, he forces runners immediately ahead of him to advance as well.

Rules of a force play. Under normal circumstances, a runner must be tagged to be put out. However, when a runner is forced to advance, a fielder needs only to tag the base that the runner is attempting to reach in order to put him out.

The cause of a force play

The "forced run" takes place when a runner must vacate a base in order to make room for a batter-runner or another runner immediately behind him.

The force begins with a batter who is attempting to reach first base. If a batter gets a hit, he has no other option but to advance to first base. He is forced to run. Because he

is forced, the fielders need only to tag first base to retire the batter-runner.

If there is a runner occupying first base when the batter gets a hit, that runner must also advance in order to make room for the forced batter. This has a domino effect — all runners occupying a base immediately in front of another forced runner must also advance.

A force occurs only when the runner has no choice but to advance.

For example, if a runner attempts to steal second base, he will not force a runner ahead of him to advance. This is because the runner trying to steal the base is not forced to steal, so he can't force a runner ahead of him.

Example: A basic force play – the force double play

---

1. With a runner on first base, the batter hits the ball sharply toward second base. Both runners must advance.

The force play is on. Both runners are forced to run, and either one can be put out if a fielder tags the runner's base before he reaches it.

---

2. The second baseman tags second base to retire the lead runner.

The lead runner is out. Since he is forced by the batter-runner, he is out if the fielder tags the base before he reaches it.

---

3. The second baseman throws the ball to the first baseman who tags first base.

The batter-runner is out. Because he is a forced runner, the batter is out when the first baseman tags first base. This very common play is called a "force double play."

Force Plays | # Force Plays Can Be Removed

The force play is off when the runner behind him is put out.

When two or more runners are being forced, it is because the lead runner needs to make room for the runner behind him. The force play is removed when the runner immediately behind a forced runner is put out. There is no longer any need to make room, so the runner is no longer forced to advance.

A force situation is over when his base is reached

The force situation is over as soon as the runner touches the base to which he was forced. For instance, if a batter reaches first base safely and chooses to continue to second base, the force play is off after he passes first base. The runner has the option to remain on first base, therefore he is not forced to advance to second.

However, if the same runner (for whatever reason) retreats back past first base towards home plate, the force play is back in effect as soon as he recrosses first base.

Example: **The force play is removed when the preceding runner is put out.**

---

1. With a runner on first base, the batter hits the ball toward the pitcher. Both the batter and the runner must run.

The force play is on. The batter and the runner are forced to run, and either one can be put out if a fielder tags his base before he reaches it.

---

2. The pitcher throws the ball to the first baseman who steps on first base to put out the batter-runner.

The force at second is off The batter-runner is out because he is a forced runner. As soon as he is out, the lead runner is no longer forced to advance to second.

---

3. The first baseman throws the ball to the second baseman who tags second base. The runner slides into second without being tagged.

The runner is safe. Since there is no longer a force play in effect on the lead runner, he cannot be put out unless he is tagged.

A reverse force double play

The situation above is called a reverse force double play because the force is removed from the lead runner as soon as the batter-runner is put out. In our example however, the reverse force double play was not completed.

Force Plays | ## Force Plays Can Be Removed

continued

Example: The force play is removed as soon as the runner passes the base.

---

1. With a runner on first base, the batter gets a hit to deep left field. Both the batter and the runner must advance.

The force play is on.
The batter and the runner are forced to run, and either one can be put out if a fielder tags his base before he reaches it.

---

2. The batter makes it safely to first base and continues to second base. The lead runner makes it to second and continues toward third base.

The force play is off.
As soon as the runners pass the bases to which they are forced, the force plays are removed.

---

3. The runners change their minds and scramble back to first and second bases. In his haste, while retreating back to second, the runner overruns the base, ending up between first and second base. At the same time, the second baseman catches the ball and tags second base.

The force play is back on, and the lead runner is out. As soon as the runner recrosses second base, the base to which he was originally forced, the force play is again in effect. At this point, the second baseman only needs to tag second base to put out the lead runner.

Force Plays | ## Forced by an Awarded Base

Forced by a walk or any awarded bases

When a batter or runner is awarded a base, runners directly in front of him will also be allowed to advance without risk of being put out. They are, in effect, forced to advance by the runner or batter who was awarded the base or bases.

If a runner advances beyond his awarded base, he can be put out if the ball is still live.

For instance, a batter gets a base-on-balls, forcing a runner on first base to advance to second. The lead runner carelessly walks past second base toward third base. The alert pitcher throws the ball to the second baseman who tags the runner for an out.

Since the runner moved past the base to which he was allowed to advance, he is no longer protected by the awarded base.

Base Running Mistakes

Overview: This section is about the many ways the offensive team can be penalized when a runner makes a mistake. It includes a mishaps such as passing another runner, missing a base, or failing to tag up.

Mistakes	**Missing a Base**

Bases must be touched in order.

While running the bases, a runner must touch all the bases he passes in order. If he fails to touch one of the bases, the defensive team can put him out by either tagging the runner or the by tagging the base that was missed.

The runner can also be put out after the play is over by making an appeal. The appeal is made by tagging the runner or by tagging the missed base.

Going back to retouch a missed base

The runner may return to retouch a base that he missed under the following circumstances:

- **During a play** he may return to retouch a missed base, but as he returns, he must touch each base in reverse order.

- **When the ball is dead** he can only return to a missed base if he has not yet reached the next base. For example, if a runner misses second

base during a home run trot around the bases, he can no longer return to retouch second base once he steps on third base.

Note: A runner may no longer return to a missed base after a runner behind him scores. For instance, if a runner fails to touch home plate, and a runner behind him reaches home plate before he can retouch it, the first runner may no longer return to touch home plate. He can be called out by appeal.

Example: Missing a base

With a runner on first base, the batter hits a fly ball deep into the outfield. Thinking the ball will not be caught, the runner runs past second toward third base.

The left fielder catches the ball for an out, and the runner must return to first base before being tagged.

The runner makes it back to first base, but failed to touch second base on the way there.

The defensive team may put out the runner by tagging him or tagging second base (the base he missed).

Note: If a runner misses home plate, he may attempt to retouch it before a fielder tags him. If, however, the runner begins to walk from the base toward the dugout (either believing or bluffing that he touched the base safely), the fielder with the ball can tag home plate to make the out, even though it is not a force situation.

Mistakes | ## Missing or Passing an Awarded Base

Missing an awarded base

When a runner is awarded bases, he still must touch the bases in order — even if the ball is dead.

Example: A runner who is awarded third base can be put out on appeal if he fails to touch second base on his way to third.

Moving past the awarded base

When a runner is awarded bases he is allowed to advance without risk of being put out. However, while the ball is in play, if a runner overruns the base to which he is awarded, he may be put out. He will lose his immunity as soon as he moves past the base.

Example: A batter walks with a runner on first base. The runner on first base is entitled to advance to second base. After reaching second base, the runner thoughtlessly steps off the base toward third, and the alert second baseman tags him with the ball. Even though he was awarded second base without liability to be put out, the runner can be tagged out as soon as he passes that base.

Mistakes | ## Failing to Tag Up Before Advancing

If a batter hits a fair or foul ball that is caught for an out, following the catch the runner can touch his original base and then attempt to advance to the next base.

Therefore the runner can either wait at the base until the fielder catches the ball, or he can retouch the base after the ball is caught.

Sometimes a runner will leave the base too early, or fail to retouch the base after the catch. If the runner fails to tag up, he can be put out during the play when a fielder holding the ball tags him or his original base.

See a full description of "Tagging Up" on page 112.

Mistakes | ## Appeal Plays and "Fourth Outs"

An appeal play can result in a "fourth out." If a third out is made but at the same time a violation by another runner takes place that results in an appeal, the out called as a result of the appeal counts as the third out. In cases where two separate appeal plays take place but only one is needed to

end the half-inning, the defense can choose to accept the out that is to its advantage.

Example: With two outs, the batter gets a hit, and two base runners advance to home plate. The first runner misses the base but the second runner touches it. An instant later, the batter-runner is

thrown out at second for the third out. At this point, both runs count. However, after the play, the first runner is called out by appeal, and his run no longer counts. Since the first runner's out ended the inning, the second run will no longer count either. See "Scoring with Two Outs" on page 113.

Mistakes | Abandoning the Bases

It is in the team's best interest for a runner to try to make it safely to the next base. In fact, its against the rules to give up this attempt and walk away.

If a base runner leaves the bases before the end of the inning or before being called out, he will be called out by the umpire for "abandoning his effort to touch the next base."

Typically this infraction will be made by a runner who is somehow confused and thinks that he is out or that the inning is over, and leaves his base to return to the dugout.

This is a judgment call by the umpire, and no appeal is necessary by the defensive team. Before the call is made, the runner must walk far enough from the base to indicate to the umpire that he is abandoning further effort.

Mistakes | Overrunning First Base

When a batter runner is attempting to reach first base, typically his momentum will take him several steps past the base. This is called overrunning first base, and the runner is allowed to do so without risk of being put out, except under the following circumstances:

The runner fails to return to first base immediately.

The runner is required to return to first immediately after overrunning the base. If he fails to retouch first base quickly enough in the umpire's judgment (and doesn't call time out), a fielder will be allowed to tag him out.

The batter-runner moves toward second base.

A legal "overrun" must be in the same direction as his run to the base. It is not considered "overrunning" or "oversliding" if the batter-runner rounds first base toward second. If the umpire judges him to be intentionally moving toward second base he can be tagged out.

Mistakes | Passing a Runner or Sharing One Base

Passing a runner

This rule is very simple. A runner who passes a runner in front of him will be called out. The lead runner will be allowed to continue his attempt to advance.

Two runners occupying the same base

If two runners end up on the same base, it is the lead runner who has the right to be on the base. The runner who is following him will be called out.

This is because the lead runner is not considered to have given up his right to the base until he has been either put out or until he has successfully reached the next base.

Tagging Up: Advancing on a Caught Batted Ball

Overview: Runners are allowed to advance even when a batted ball is caught for an out. Before attempting to advance, the runner must retouch his base after the fielder touches the ball.

A runner can advance, at risk of being tagged out, after a hit ball has been caught for an out. This principle is the basis for a "sacrifice fly" — where a batter hits a fly ball to the outfield. Even though he will be out if the ball is caught, a runner can tag up and advance to the next base.

The rule. The runner must touch his original base after the hit ball is touched by the fielder. That means he can wait on his base and begin running once the fielder touches the ball, or he can retouch the base at any time after the fielder touches the ball before advancing to the next base.

Example: Tagging up

1. The ball is hit. The runner stays on his base and readies himself to run.

2. The ball is caught. The runner must be touching the base at the time of the catch. If not, he must retouch it after the catch.

3. The runner is allowed to advance. The runner will try to leave the base as quickly as possible after the ball is touched by the fielder.

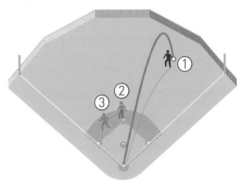

Note: On a high fly ball, the runner will act like a track sprinter waiting for the pistol to signal the start of a race. He will begin running the instant that the ball is touched.

Tagging Up | **Failing to Tag Up**

Sometimes a runner can be caught off the base, or will have begun his run thinking that the ball will not be caught. If a fair ball is caught for an out, a runner must retouch his base before he attempts to advance.

If a runner fails to tag up, he can be put out in the following ways:

Tagging the runner. A runner who fails to retouch his original base can be tagged out at anytime during a live play.

Tagging the original base. If a runner needs to retouch his original base, it is treated like a force play in which the runner has no choice but to reach the base. As in the case of a force play, the runner can be put out when a fielder tags the base in question.

By appeal. If the defensive team feels that a runner left his base before a fly ball was caught, they can make an appeal after the play is over by throwing the ball to his original base or by tagging the runner.

Example: Failing to tag up

A batter hits a line drive, and a runner on first base, thinking the ball will go over the first baseman's head for a hit, begins running as soon as the ball leaves the bat.

The hit is caught by the leaping first baseman as the runner approaches second base.

At this point, the runner must return to first base. He may not proceed to second because he didn't touch first base after the catch. The first baseman tags first base and the runner is out.

A touch is close enough.

The rule book states that runners may not advance until the fielder actually catches the ball, and a catch is officially defined as having controlled possession of the ball.

However, in a tag-up situation the runners are allowed to advance as soon as the fielder touches the ball, even if the fielder juggles or bobbles the ball before gaining full control.

This prevents the fielder from intentionally juggling the ball while walking towards the infield in order to keep the runners on their bases.

Scoring with Two Outs

Overview: A run scored during a play in which the third out is made may or may not count depending on the circumstances.

When the run does not count

The run will not count if a runner crosses home plate on a play in which the third out is made, under the following circumstances:

- the batter-runner is called out before he reaches first base.
- a runner is forced out.
- a runner in front of the scoring run missed one of the bases.

The winning run

If the winning run is made because a batter is awarded a base (by being walked or hit by a pitch for instance), and the bases are loaded, the game will not end until:

- the batter touches first base.
- the runner at third touches home plate.

If one or both runners take too much time to touch their bases (perhaps because they are too busy celebrating) the umpire will call the culprit out and resume the game.

Exception: If the fans mob the field and prevent the runners from reaching their bases, the umpire will ignore the infraction. The run will score.

Running Outside the Base Path

Overview: Under normal circumstances, it is not against the rules for a runner to stray outside the base path. He is only penalized if he does so intentionally to avoid a tag or to interfere with a play.

Avoiding a tag

A runner must not stray more than three feet to either side of a direct line between the bases when trying to avoid a tag.

Penalty: The runner will be called out.

Exception: It is okay (and may even be necessary) to run outside the baseline to avoid interfering with a fielder who is actively making a play on a batted ball.

Interfering with a play at first base

Normally a runner is allowed to use the entire six foot width of the base path, but the rules are a little more constraining for a batter-runner on his way to first base.

While a play is being attempted at first base, after the batter-runner has passed more than half the distance to first base, he must stay within an area three feet to the right of the foul line, and he must not cross to the left of the foul line.

Penalty: The ball is dead, and the runner will be called out.

Running to first base. While running to first base, the batter-runner must stay out of the way of a play being made at first. After reaching the halfway point he must run in the area of the base path outside of the foul line.

Interfering with a double play

Interference is called when a runner veers outside of the base path in order to interfere with a fielder attempting a double play.

Between first and second bases, and second and third, there are no clear demarcations for the boundaries of the base path.

An umpire will judge a runner to be within the base path if he can reach it with his hand or foot as he slides by. See page 120.

Touched By a Batted Ball

Overview: If a batted ball hits a runner or umpire, it could hinder or prevent a fielder from making a play. The rules address this situation differently depending on the circumstances under which the player or umpire is touched by the ball.

Explanation: The most basic issue surrounding this rule is whether the runner or umpire is touched before or after the ball gets past a fielder.

If the contact is made before passing a fielder, then the ball is dead and the umpire must address the incident.

If the ball makes contact after a fielder has already missed the ball and has let it get by him, then the play will continue as if the incident did not occur.

Like many rules in baseball, it isn't quite that simple. There are a few more circumstances to consider. Refer to the specific examples and circumstances below.

A runner is touched by a hit before it passes a fielder.

What happens: The runner is out, and the batter will be awarded first base.

The ball is dead, and no other runners score or advance unless they are forced to advance by the batter.

Example: A ball is hit hard and grazes the runner, who has a lead off second base, before any fielder can attempt to catch the ball.

Note: In the rare event that two runners are touched by the same fair ball, the first runner will be the one called out. The ball becomes instantly dead after touching the first runner.

A runner is touched by a hit that gets past a fielder.

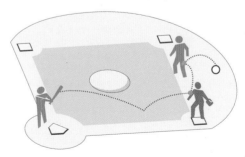

Explanation: There is no penalty if a fair ball deflects off or gets past a fielder as he attempts to catch it, and it touches a runner immediately behind him.

In this case the play continues as if nothing happened.

Example: A ball is hit hard toward the first baseman with a runner on his way to second. The ball deflects off the first baseman and touches the runner.

What happens: The ball remains in play as if the incident did not occur. All runners, including the batter, will continue to advance at risk.

Note: If the umpire decides that the runner purposely kicked or deflected the ball, the runner will be called out on interference.

Touched By a Batted Ball

continued

A runner is touched by a batted ball while in front of a fielder making a play.

Explanation: If a runner touches a batted ball while directly in front a fielder attempting to make a play, the ball is dead and the runner is out — even if it already touched or got past another fielder.

Example: The ball is hit hard toward the pitcher with a runner on his way to third. The ball deflects off the pitcher then touches the runner.

The third baseman is behind the runner and may have been able to field the ball if it hadn't touched the runner.

What happens: the runner is out, and the batter will be awarded first base.

The ball is dead, and no other runners score or advance unless they are forced to advance by the batter.

A batted ball is deflected by fielder, bounces off a runner, and is then caught by another fielder.

Explanation: Once the ball bounces off the runner, it is treated as if it had touched the ground, so it is no longer a fly ball.

Note: If the ball is deflected off the runner in a way that prevents the second baseman from making a play on the ball, the runner may be called out for interference.

Example: A ball is hit to the pitcher who deflects the ball towards a runner going to second base. The ball bounces off the runner into the hands of the second baseman, without yet touching the ground.

What happens: The catch doesn't count. The ball remains in play as if the incident did not occur.

All runners (including the batter) will continue to advance at risk.

Touched By a Hit	An Umpire Is Touched By a Batted Ball

With a few exceptions, these rules are very similar to those addressing a runner who is touched by a batted ball. Many of the diagrams found in the previous section could help to clarify the following circumstances.

Touched by a hit before it passes a fielder

If a fair ball touches an umpire before it touches or passes by a fielder:

- the ball is dead.
- the batter advances to first base.

- no other runners score or advance unless they are forced to advance by the batter.

Touched by a hit that gets past a fielder — except the pitcher

The ball is in play if a fair ball touches an umpire after having passed through, or close to a fielder who was trying to stop the ball. The pitcher is not included in this case.

- The play continues as if the incident didn't occur.

Touched by a hit that gets past the pitcher

There are two conditions by which this will happen:

If the ball does not touch the pitcher, bouncing over or continuing past the pitcher, and the ball touches an umpire:

- the ball is dead.
- the batter is awarded first base.

If the ball does touch the pitcher, gets past him and then touches the umpire:

- the play continues as if the incident didn't occur.

Interference and Obstruction

Overview: Interference occurs when a runner or batter gets in the way of a fielder who is trying to make a play. Obstruction occurs when a fielder gets in the way of a runner who is trying to advance or return to a base.

Interference and obstruction

Interference in baseball is a general term that is applied to a variety of actions made against the defensive and offensive teams. Most often, however, it is used to describe an action by a member of the offensive team who hinders a fielder's attempt at making a play.

The act of interference could include physical contact with the fielder or the ball, or an attempt to confuse or distract a fielder who is making a play.

Obstruction describes an act that adversely affects a runner — when a fielder unfairly blocks or impedes a runner's advance during a play.

Interference and obstruction can be difficult judgment calls for the umpire to make. For either interference or obstruction to be called, the umpire must determine whether the outcome of the play was affected by the action. With a few exceptions, interference or obstruction is not called unless the act prevents a fielder

from completing a play or a runner from reaching a base.

Example: A runner on his way to third base goes out of his way to shove the shortstop. The ball is thrown by the right fielder to the third baseman, but the throw arrives too late and the runner is safe.

Although this was a blatant act, in this case, there is no interference because the shortstop was not part of the play. The runner's shove had no effect on the outcome, so the play stands.

Interference and Obstruction

continued

However, after the play is completed, the umpire may warn or even eject the runner from the game for his conduct.

Who has right of way?

The runner normally has right of way on the base paths, but the fielder has right of way while in the act of making a play on a batted ball.

Example: Interference.
A fielder dives in front of a runner in an attempt to catch a batted ball. The runner collides with the fielder, who misses the catch. Interference is called against the runner.

Example: Obstruction.
A fielder dives into the path of a runner to catch a ball. He misses the ball and does not immediately move to get out of the runner's way. The runner collides with the fielder and is unable to reach his base as a result. Obstruction is called against the fielder.

Is it a batted or thrown ball?

A fielder only has right of way over the runner if he is in the act of fielding a *batted* ball. If he's trying to catch a *thrown* ball, he has a right to be in the base path, but the runner is under no obligation to avoid him. If a collision occurs under these circumstances, there will be no penalty called against either party unless the umpire feels that one of the players intentionally or unnecessarily caused the contact.

Similarly, if a fielder has possession of the ball and stands in the way of the runner in order to tag him, the runner is allowed to run into the fielder in his attempt to reach the base. If the fielder drops the ball as a result of the contact, the runner will be safe. This type of incident is often seen when a runner collides with a catcher who is trying to block home plate.

Example: Collision at home plate. During the 1951 World Series, the umpire changed his call to safe when Alvin Dark of the Giants collided with Yogi Berra of the Yankees, causing him to drop the ball. Since both had a right to the base path, neither obstruction or interference was called.

Interference by a Runner

Overview: When a runner interferes with a fielder or a ball in play, he will be called out as a penalty. A runner and the batter will both be called out if the interference was judged to have prevented a double play.

The runner is out:

- if a runner interferes with a fielder making a play on a batted ball, whether intentional or not.

  Exception: If a runner is touching a base when he interferes with the fielder, the umpire must determine that the interference was intentional before making the call.

- if a runner interferes with or is touched by a batted ball before it touches or goes past a fielder. In this case, it doesn't matter if the incident was intentional or not.

- if a batted ball gets past a fielder (whether or not he touched it), and the runner intentionally kicks or deflects the ball. See "Touched by a Batted Ball" on pages 115 and 116.

- if a runner intentionally interferes with a batted ball by throwing his helmet, bat, or any object at or in the path of the ball.

- if a runner intentionally interferes with a thrown ball.

- if a runner runs outside the base path to interfere with a play, on a thrown or batted ball. See "Running Outside the Base Path" on page 114.

Note: If there is contact between the batter-runner and the catcher, while the batter-runner is on his way to first base and the catcher is fielding the hit ball, the umpire will rarely call interference unless the infraction is blatant or extreme.

The ball is dead, and no runners may advance.

When there are other runners who are not involved with the interference, they will be made to return to the last base they touched before the interference occurred (referred to as the "time of interference").

Exception: If the interference occurs before the batter-runner reaches first base, all runners will return to the base they occupied before the pitch was made.

Note: In a case in which two or more fielders are attempting to field the same ball, interference will only be called if it is committed against the fielder who, in the judgment of the umpire, is entitled to the ball.

Example: Two fielders are trying to catch a ground ball. At the last second, one of them abandons his attempt to field the ball and steps out of the way of the other fielder but directly in front of a runner. Even if the ball is dropped in the confusion, there will be no call of interference because the contact was on the fielder who was not "entitled" to the ball. In fact, that fielder could be called for obstruction.

Interference | On a Double Play

Runner interferes with a throw on a double play

If a runner intentionally interferes with a fielder's throw as he is attempting to make a double play, both the runner and the batter will be called out — the runner for interfering with the double play and the batter under the assumption that the fielder may have been able to complete the double play.

It's common to see a runner veer toward the fielder in a double play situation. In fact it is considered good base running and is encouraged by the offensive team. The important thing is to remain within the base path in order to avoid a call of interference.

This type of interference is a tricky judgment call, and generally the runner is given ample leeway.

If the runner interferes:

- the runner and the batter are out.
- the ball is dead.
- no runners may advance or score as the result of the interference.

Runner or batter interferes with a batted ball on a double play

Both the runner and the batter will be out if either of them intentionally interferes with a batted ball or a fielder attempting to field a batted ball during a possible double play.

If the runner interferes:

- the runner and the batter are out.
- the ball is dead.
- no other runners will be allowed to advance on the play.

If the batter interferes:

- the batter and the runner closest to home plate are out.
- the ball is dead.
- no other runners will be allowed to advance on the play.

Note: The rule states that the batter and the runner closest to home should be called out in this case, even if the double play would have been made on another runner. The idea is to penalize the offence by removing the more valuable runner — the one closest to home plate.

Interference with two outs

If there are already two outs when the interference occurs, only the batter will be called out, ending the inning.

Example: Interference on a double play

It's very common to see a runner sliding directly toward a fielder who is trying to complete a double play.

Typically an umpire will not call interference unless the runner has strayed so far from the base that he can no longer reach it with his hand or foot as he slides by.

Note: The runner is not allowed to try to block the throw by raising his hands or throwing his body in the way of the throw.

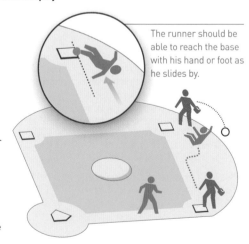

The runner should be able to reach the base with his hand or foot as he slides by.

Interference | # By a Coach or Teammate

There are several situations in which a runner will be called out due to the actions of his teammates, including a coach or the batter.

Interference by a teammate

All members of the offensive team are required to stay clear of a fielder in the act of fielding the ball. This includes team members on the sidelines, who must clear the dugout if a fielder needs that space.

As penalty for a team member or members not avoiding the fielder, the batter or runner involved in the play will be called out.

Teammates cannot gather around a base.

A runner's teammates are not permitted to gather near a base to which the runner is advancing for the purpose of distracting or confusing a fielder attempting to make a play. As a penalty the runner will be called out due to interference by his teammates.

A coach cannot touch a runner.

The first base coach or third base coach must never touch a runner to assist him in any way. As a penalty the runner will be called out.

Example: A runner is rounding third base and is planning on continuing to home plate. The third base coach sees that a throw being made to home is likely to put him out at the plate. The coach cannot grab or hold the runner in an effort to make him stop on third.

A coach interferes with a fielder.

A coach must never leave the coach's box in order to affect a fielder's throw or a play on the ball.

Batter interference at home plate

With less than two outs and a runner on third base, the batter must not intentionally hinder a fielder making a play at home base. If he does, the runner will be called out even though it was the batter's fault. The idea is to penalize the offensive team by removing the more valuable player — the runner at third base.

If this occurs when there are already two outs, the batter, not the runner, will be charged with the third out.

Interference by a batter or runner who has been put out

A batter or runner who has just been put out must not interfere with a subsequent attempt to put out a second runner, for example, by trying to confuse or physically interfere with a fielder. If he does, the second runner will also be called out due to his teammate's action.

Note: It is not considered interference if the batter or runner who has just been put out continues to advance to the next base — for instance, if he did not realize he had been put out. This does not constitute an attempt to confuse the fielders or hinder a play.

Did he do it on purpose?

When it comes to interference by a non-player, the umpire must decide whether or not the interference was intentional.

Example: A first base coach rolls to the ground to avoid a thrown ball. The first baseman trips over the coach while trying to retrieve the ball. During the ensuing confusion, the batter-runner makes it all the way to third base.

It would be tempting for the umpire to automatically call interference on the coach, but if he feels that the coach was honestly trying to avoid the ball and never intended to get in the way of the fielder, he must not call interference. The play must stand.

Interference | ## By an Umpire or a Spectator

In certain situations an umpire or spectator may interfere with a live ball or with a fielder attempting to make a play. The following describes the effect these different types of interference have on a base runner.

If an umpire interferes with a catcher

If an umpire gets in the way of a catcher attempting to prevent a stolen base, the ball is dead and all runners must return to their bases. If the catcher is able to throw the runner out despite the interference, then the incident will be disregarded.

If an umpire is touched by a fair ball before it passes a fielder

In this case:

- the batter will be awarded first base.
- the ball is dead.
- no other runners score or advance unless they are forced to advance by the batter.

See "Touched by a Batted Ball" on page 116 for more information.

Spectator interference

It is considered spectator interference if a spectator reaches out of the stands, or if he falls or steps out of the stands onto the playing field, and interferes with the fielder or touches a live ball.

If this occurs:

- the ball is dead.
- the umpire will take actions, such as calling runners out or awarding bases, to minimize or nullify the impact of the spectator's interference.

See "Spectator Interference" on page 182 for more information.

Obstruction on a Runner

Overview: Obstruction occurs when a fielder who does not have possession of the ball or is not actively fielding the ball impedes a runner who is trying to advance or retreat on the bases.

Like interference, obstruction is a judgment call by the umpire. If there's contact between a runner and a fielder, the umpire must determine whether or not the fielder had a right to be in that particular spot at the time of contact.

If the fielder is making a play on a batted ball, he has right of way.

If the fielder is not actively making a play on a ball, the runner has right of way in the base path.

What defines "the act of making a play"

If a fielder is about to catch a ball, and the ball is moving towards him at a speed and direction that demands him to be at a certain location on the field, then the fielder is "in the act of making a play." He has a right to be in that location.

Obstruction must have an impact on the play.

In order to qualify as obstruction the action must have had an impact on the play. If the runner is obstructed but he makes it safely to the base he would have reached had the obstruction not occurred, then the incident will be ignored.

Contact is not always obstruction or interference.

There are only a few circumstances in which a fielder might block a runner in the base paths, and only one of these situations constitutes obstruction. The following is a list of circumstances where contact could be made between runner and fielder.

No obstruction. The fielder is trying to field a *batted* ball. In this case, the fielder has right of way, and the runner may be charged with interference if contact is made.

No obstruction. The fielder is trying to field a *thrown* ball. The fielder has a right to be in the path of the runner if the umpire feels he must be there in order to field the ball. However, the runner also has a right to the base path and is not required to get out of the fielder's way. Even if there is a major collision, neither obstruction nor interference will be called unless the umpire judges one of the players to be unnecessarily impeding the other.

No obstruction. With possession of the ball, the fielder is trying to tag a runner. As in the case of a fielder trying to catch a thrown ball, both the runner and the fielder have a right to be in the same location. Neither obstruction nor interference will be called unless the umpire judges one of the players to be unnecessarily impeding the other.

Obstruction. The fielder does not have possession of the ball and is not actively fielding the ball. This is the only instance when the fielder will be called for obstruction due to contact with the runner.

Obstruction called on a fielder who has right of way

In rare situations an umpire may call obstruction on a fielder who is making a play and has the right of way if the fielder unnecessarily impedes the runner.

The violation would have to be obvious and flagrant to earn the call. For instance, the fielder would have to intentionally punch, trip, or kick the runner.

Obstruction | ## Immediate vs. Delayed Dead Ball

An immediate dead ball

When a runner is obstructed while fielders are attempting to put him out, or when the batter is obstructed before he reaches first base, the umpire will call obstruction immediately. The ball will be dead the instant the call is made.

A delayed dead ball

If there is no play being made on the obstructed runner, and the batter-runner has already reached first base at the time of obstruction, the umpire will allow the play to continue until all action stops. This is known as a delayed dead ball.

When the play is complete, the umpire will decide if the obstruction had any impact on the outcome of the play. If the runner is obstructed, but all runners make it safely to the bases they would have reached had the obstruction not occurred, the obstruction will be ignored.

If the umpire believes that the obstruction prevented any of the runners from safely advancing, he will award bases to runners in an effort to nullify the effects of the obstruction.

Note: If during a play in which obstruction has been called, a runner advances beyond the base that he would be awarded due to the obstruction, he does so at risk and may be tagged out.

9 | Fielding

A baseball defense is composed of nine fielders who will do anything (within the rules) to prevent the offense from scoring. This chapter discusses the ways a fielder can put out a batter or a runner. It also discusses violations of the rules by fielders that can have the opposite effect — runners can be awarded bases.

Fielding: contents

Basics for the Fielder

Overview: A fielder's job is to put out three offensive players before their team can score a run. Fielders hope to prevent batters from reaching first base and prevent runners from advancing to their next base. All nine defensive players, including the pitcher and catcher, are considered fielders.

Note: The pitcher is, technically, one of the nine fielders. There are enough rules on pitching however for the pitcher to merit his own chapter. The rules regarding the catcher and the other seven fielders (and just a few references to rules concerning the pitcher) are covered here.

Positions of the nine fielders

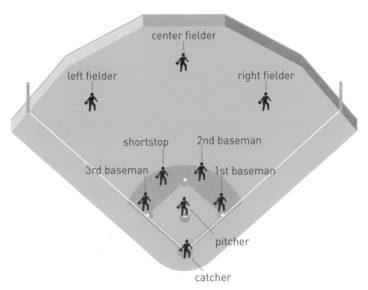

Distance of a typical throw from outfielder to infielder to home plate.

Basics	# Fielding

Fielders must be in fair territory when the umpire calls "play."

The nine fielders are:

- pitcher
- catcher
- first baseman
- second baseman
- shortstop
- third baseman
- right fielder
- center fielder
- left fielder

At the start of the game, and anytime the umpire calls "play" during the game, the catcher must be in his position in the catcher's box behind home plate, and the pitcher will be in his position on the pitcher's plate. The other seven fielders must be positioned in fair territory.

While the fielders are each assigned specific locations on the field, the pitcher and the catcher are the only fielders required by the rules to be in specific locations — and this is only required at the time of the pitch. The other seven fielders may position themselves anywhere in fair territory. The seven "standard" positions, shown in the diagram

at left, are universally accepted, assuring that both the infield and outfield are adequately covered, but they are not required by the rules.

Exception: None of the fielders can position himself between the pitcher and the catcher, blocking the batter's view of the pitch. Fielders must also stay out of the way of base runners unless they are in the act of making a play. See "Obstruction on a Runner" on page 122.

The Pitcher: Some rules pertaining to fielders are different for the pitcher.

Most rules covered in this chapter pertain to all nine fielders. However, although the pitcher is technically a fielder, when performing his role as a pitcher some rules are different.

An example is the rule regarding **wild throws**. If a pitcher makes a wild throw, to first base for instance, and that throw goes into the stands or elsewhere out of play, the batter and all runners will be allowed to advance one base (awarded one base). If a fielder does the same, the batter and all runners will be awarded two bases each, not one.

A pitcher "stops" being a pitcher, and is treated like another fielder when:

1. the pitcher disengages from the pitcher's plate.

2. the pitcher completes his pitch.

When pitching, the pitcher must assume his legal pitching position. Early in his pitching sequence the pitcher may decide to step off of the pitcher's plate, "disengaging" the plate. If he does, he is governed by the rules regarding fielders.

This means that immediately following the pitch, the pitcher may cover any location on the field just like any other fielder. Once he stops being a pitcher, all fielder's rules apply (see the Pitching chapter, page 64).

The Catcher: The catcher is not confined to the catcher's box.

The only time the catcher is required to be in the catcher's box is when the umpire calls "play." Otherwise, to catch a pitch or to make a play, his position is not restricted. He can be anywhere on the field.

Exception: When the pitcher is intentionally delivering a base-on-balls (a "walk") the catcher must have both feet within the catcher's box at the time the ball leaves the pitcher's hand. If he fails to do this, or if the pitcher makes his pitch before the catcher has a chance to position his feet inside the catcher's box, the pitcher will be charged with a balk.

Awarded Bases Due to a Fielder

Overview: Sometimes, a fielder's attempts at preventing a runner from advancing can have the opposite affect. The following is a list of all the ways a runner can be awarded bases due to actions of a fielder.

Awarded Bases	One Base is Awarded....

1. if a fielder falls into the dugout or stands after catching a fly ball, the batter will be out and all runners will be awarded one base. The ball is dead. If the fielder remains standing however, the ball remains live, unless he entered a spectator area.

2. if a catcher or other fielder interferes with a batter stealing first base, all runners will be awarded one base.

Awarded Bases	Two Bases Are Awarded...

1. if a fielder intentionally touches a thrown ball with his cap or any piece of his uniform or equipment detached from his body — for instance, if he tries to catch a thrown ball with his cap. The batter and all runners advance two bases. The ball remains in play.

2. if a fielder intentionally throws his glove or cap at a thrown ball or any piece of his uniform or equipment. The batter and all runners advance two bases. The ball remains in play.

Note: In instances where the ball is touched by a detached glove, cap, piece of uniform or equipment unintentionally, the bases will not be awarded. For instance, if a fielder is running to make a catch, he jumps while reaching up, his glove flies off of his hand from the momentum of his arm's movement, and the glove touches the ball, it would be considered unintentional — bases would not be awarded.

3. if a fair ball deflects off of a fielder and goes out of play. If the deflected ball goes into the stands beyond the first or third base foul line, or if the ball either goes under, though, or becomes stuck in a fence, scoreboard, shrubbery, or vines, two bases are awarded.

4. if a fielder makes a wild throw and the ball goes out of play. If the throw puts the ball in the stands, into the bench or dugout, or it goes over, under, though, or becomes stuck in a fence, two bases are awarded. The ball is dead.

If the wild throw was made on the first play after the ball was hit, the two bases will be awarded according to the position of the runners at the time of the pitch. Otherwise, the two bases will be awarded according to the position of the batter and runners at the time the ball left the fielder's hand.

Note: In some cases this will make it impossible to award each runner two bases, since two runners may be between the same two bases. For example, it is possible for two runners to be between second and third base when the wild throw takes place. If this occurs, one of the runners will be awarded only one base, since two runners cannot occupy the same base and no runner can advance more than two bases under this rule.

Awarded Bases	Three Bases Are Awarded....

1. **if a fielder intentionally touches a batted, fair ball with his cap** or any piece of his uniform or equipment detached from his body — for instance, if he tries to catch a batted ball with his cap. All runners advance to home to score, and

the batter advances three bases. The ball remains in play.

2. **if a fielder intentionally throws his glove or cap at a fair batted ball** or throws any piece of his uniform or equipment at a batted, fair

ball. All runners advance to home to score, and the batter advances to third base. The ball remains in play.

Awarded bases	Home Runs Are Awarded....

1. **if a fly ball is deflected by a fielder and goes into the stands or over a fence in fair territory,** the batter and all runners advance to home to score.

Example: A center fielder runs to the wall to make a catch that would have hit the wall. In reaching up to

make the catch, the ball bounces off of his glove and goes over the fence. The batter is awarded a home run.

2. **if a fly ball that would have been a home run is deflected.** If, in the umpire's judgment, a hit would have gone into the

stands or over a fence in fair territory for a home run, but it was deflected because a fielder threw his glove, cap or any piece of his uniform or equipment at it, the batter and all runners advance to home to score.

Many uses for the term "tag"

Tag has several uses. **1.** A batter or runner tags his base when he touches it — usually with his foot, but sometimes also with his hand if sliding head-first into the base. Any body part can be used to tag the base. **2.** It also refers to a fielder, with the ball in his possession, touching a base. (Without the ball, a fielder touching a base means nothing.) **3.** Lastly, a fielder can tag the batter or runner himself. With the ball in his hand or in his glove, the fielder can use that hand or glove to touch the batter or runner as he is running to first, running between bases, or caught off base.

If a Fielder Enters the Stands or Dugout

If a fielder enters the stands or dugout to make a catch

A ball is legally caught even when a fielder enters the stands or dugout to make a catch. A fielder may reach, leap, or fall into the stands before or after catching the ball. If he manages to hold onto it, the catch is legal.

- **If the fielder falls into the stands or dugout** after making the catch, the ball is dead and runners are awarded one base.

- **If the fielder remains standing,** the ball remains in play. Runners may tag up (by touching their original base) and advance, at their own risk.

Obstruction by a Fielder

Overview: Runners, including a batter on his way to first base, have right-of-way when running the bases. Unless a fielder has the ball, he may not obstruct the runner, or in any way impede his progress. If he does, the following rules apply.

Obstruction of a runner

Baselines belong to the runners, not the fielders. Runners have right-of-way. Blocking the path of a runner or blocking the runner himself, without possession of the ball, is considered "obstruction." The umpire signals obstruction using the same motion he makes when calling "time" — by raising both hands over his head.

When a fielder obstructs a runner while a play is being made on the obstructed runner:

• the runner or runners are awarded the bases that the umpire believes the runners would have reached had the obstruction not occurred. The obstructed runner will therefore advance at least one base, and possibly more.

• the ball is dead when the call is made.

If a wild throw was in flight before the obstruction call was made, the wild throw rules will prevail. This can be to the advantage of the team at bat, since wild throw rules award one or two bases to each runner.

Rules concerning wild throws by fielders are discussed on page 128. For wild throws by a pitcher, see page 72.

When a fielder obstructs a runner when no play is being made on the obstructed runner:

• the umpire will let the play proceed.

• when the play is completed, the umpire will call obstruction (by signaling "time").

• the runner or runners are awarded the bases that the umpire believes the runners would have reached had the obstruction not occurred.

Gone too far? In cases where, before the ball was dead, an obstructed runner advanced to a base beyond the base he would have been awarded, and in doing so he was put out, the out will be upheld.

Obstruction at home base:

If a catcher or other fielder without the ball in his possession obstructs a runner from third base when he is:

• attempting to score by stealing home, or

• attempting to score in a squeeze play (a play in which the batter bunts in an attempt to allow a runner on third to score). Or

• if the catcher or a fielder touches the batter or his bat,

a balk will be charged against the pitcher, therefore, all runners advance one base. The batter will also be awarded first base. The ball will be dead.

All members of the offensive team, including all players and coaches, must get out of the fielder's way.

In cases where a fielder is making a play on a ball that is batted or thrown, all members of the offensive team must get out of the way. This includes players, coaches, and anyone in the dugout.

Penalty: The penalty against the offensive team for failing to get out of the way is "interference." The umpire will call out the batter or runner on whom the play was being made.

The Infield Fly Rule

Overview: If, with runners on first and second base or with the bases loaded, a fly ball is hit in or around the infield and could be easily caught by a fielder, the umpire has the option of calling the batter out before the ball is actually caught.

The intent of the rule. While it may not seem so at first, this rule is actually in the favor of the offensive team. It prevents the defensive team from intentionally dropping a fly ball in order to force the runners into an easy double play.

The result. The batter is out and the ball is still in play.

When the infield fly rule is called. The infield fly rule can only be applied under the following conditions:

- runners on first and second base or the bases loaded
- less than two outs

Example: What would happen if the infield fly rule were not called

Diagram **a** shows the situation where the infield fly rule is typically called. Diagram **b** shows the double play that could result if the infield fly rule were not called.

a. The umpire calls an infield fly when....

b. If the infield fly rule is not called, the following double play could occur....

The batter hits an infield fly that seems likely to be caught. The batter begins to run toward first base, but the runners must wait to see if the ball will be caught (see "Tagging Up" on page 112). As soon as the umpire sees that the fielder is likely to catch the ball, he will call "infield fly" to signal that the batter is out and the ball is still in play.

Offensive team: one out

The fielder intentionally drops the ball. This forces both runners to advance to the next base (see "Force Plays" on page 106).

If the infield fly had been called, they would not be forced and could remain safely on their bases.

With all runners in motion, and the ball in close proximity to the bases, the fielder can quickly pick up the ball and throw it to third and on to second for an easy double play.

Offensive team: two outs

Note: The infield fly is not in effect with only one runner on base because if the batter makes a strong effort, he will typically have time to reach first base safely. Therefore, the play will usually result in only one out.

Note: If the infield fly Rule is called and the fielder legitimately misses the catch, the batter is still out and the ball is in play.

A closely related rule

If with a runner on first base an umpire judges that a fielder intentionally dropped a fly ball after touching it, he can call the batter out after the catch is missed. This is similar to the infield fly rule, but it is called after the ball is dropped and it requires only a runner on first base.

Fielder's Choice

Overview: The term "fielder's choice" describes a play in which a fielder must choose between two or more runners, putting one of them out instead of the other.

The rules of baseball use the term fielder's choice to account for a number of situations:

1. A fielder's throw to anywhere other than first base. In this case fielder's choice refers to the decision by a fielder handling a ground ball to throw to a base other than first base, making a play on a runner other than the batter.

2. The batter's advance to first base, or beyond. In this case it accounts for the batter's actual advance to first base or beyond, following a fielder's decision to attempt to put out a runner in front of the batter instead of the batter.

3. Any runner's advance. Similar to the above, the term accounts for an advance by any runner to one or more bases, following a fielder's decision to put out a different runner. (It does not apply to runners advancing due to a stolen base or due to an error.)

4. A decision by a fielder to allow a runner to steal a base. Although not usual, in some situations the defensive team member may decide that it's okay to let a runner steal a base. Fielder's choice in this case refers to that decision.

Note: Definitions 2, 3, and 4 are typically used by the official scorekeeper.

Outs

Overview: For a fielder, some outs are more difficult than others. A fielder can actively put a batter or a runner out, or he can be credited with an "automatic" out by the official scorer.

Ways a fielder can put out a batter or a runner.

The fielder's job is to prevent a batter or runner from scoring at home plate. He does this by putting out the batter or runner, preventing runners from stealing a base, or by preventing runners from advancing whenever a ball is hit by the batter.

A fielder puts out a batter or a runner in three ways.

1. The fielder catches a fly ball hit by the batter in fair or foul territory, on a fly or a line drive (meaning he catches it before the ball has touched the ground).

2. The fielder tags a base. With the ball in his possession, the runner will be out when the fielder tags a base to which the runner is forced to advance before the runner reaches it. This includes a batter-runner who is trying to reach first base.

3. The fielder tags a runner with the ball while a runner is between bases. A fielder can put the runner out as long as the ball is in play and the runner is not touching his legal base. This includes batters running to first base.

Exception: Batters who overrun first base typically cannot be tagged out after they touch first base. See page 111 in the Running chapter.

Automatic Outs: Credits for Fielder

Overview: The official scorer, in certain cases, makes judgments about which fielder receives credit for plays that result in an automatic out.

The catcher receives credit for an automatic out on the batter when:

1. the batter illegally bats the ball. For instance, if the batter uses a bat that has been tampered with.

2. the batter bunts the ball foul on the third strike.

3. the batter is touched by the ball he batted.

4. the batter interferes with the catcher.

5. the batter misses his proper turn at bat.

6. the batter refuses to advance to first base after receiving a base-on-balls, (also called a "walk").

See the Batting chapter for more details on these rules, with examples.

The catcher receives credit for an automatic out on the runner when:

7. the runner refuses to advance from third base to home to score the winning run. (In the case of a winning run, a runner on third is required to advance. The umpire will call the runner out for refusing to run in this situation.)

The fielder receives credit for an automatic out on the batter when:

1. a batter is called out by the infield fly rule and the infield fly is not caught. The fielder who, according the official scorer, could have made the catch receives credit for the out.

This rule can lead to an odd situation. The fielder in this case could have legitimately dropped the catch, which would normally be a error. Because of the infield fly rule however, he will be automatically credited with an out.

2. the batter is called out because of interference by a runner. In a double play situation, if the runner interferes with a fielder throwing the ball or catching a thrown ball, the first baseman receives credit for the batter's automatic out. If the interfered-with fielder was throwing the ball at the time of the interference, that fielder will receive credit for an assist.

The fielder receives credit for an automatic out on the runner when:

3. a runner is touched by a batted ball. The fielder closest to the ball receives credit for the out.

4. a runner is called out for running out of the baseline to avoid being tagged. The fielder whom the runner avoided receives credit for the out.

5. a runner is called out for running past the runner in front of him. The fielder nearest the runner when he passed the preceding runner receives credit for the out.

6. a runner is called out for running the bases in reverse order, with the intent of confusing the fielders. The fielder who was covering the base from which the runner began the reverse run receives credit for the out.

7. a runner is called out for interfering with a fielder. The fielder with whom he interfered receives credit for the out. However, if the fielder was making a throw when the interference occurred, the fielder who was receiving the throw receives credit for the out. The fielder making the throw receives credit for an "assist."

10 | **Umpires**

Umpires are the official representatives of Major League Baseball. In addition to officiating, they are responsible for upholding the dignity of the game.

A typical game is overseen by an umpire-in-chief and three field umpires.

Umpires have tasks to perform before, during, and after the game. Their responsibilities range from preparing the baseballs to ejecting players after a brawl. Here are their tasks as identified in the official rules.

Umpires: contents

Basics for Umpires

Overview: Umpires are appointed by the league president, who is responsible for assigning one or more umpires to officiate at each game. Umpires are representatives of the league, and the sport of baseball itself. Their job is to uphold the rules of the game. Additionally, umpires are responsible for maintaining proper conduct on the field throughout the game.

While the official rules of baseball cover many aspects of the game, each umpire has the authority to rule over situations not mentioned in the official rules.

Members of either team, including players, coaches, managers, and team officers, must not do anything to prevent an umpire from performing his job. The umpire may enforce penalties, as appropriate.

An umpire's first rule

The first and most important rule for umpires, important enough to be printed in all capital letters in the official rules of baseball, states: BE IN POSITION TO SEE EVERY PLAY. This, of course, is mandatory if an umpire is to call a play correctly. It will also reduce objections and arguments from players who may otherwise not believe the umpire was in a good position to see what actually happened.

Positions of the umpires

A typical umpiring team consists of the umpire-in-chief, positioned at home plate (also referred to as the "plate umpire") and three field umpires. The three field umpires are responsible for specific areas of the field just like defensive players. Like fielders, umpires will shift positions depending on the circumstances. They try to be in the spot that will let them see the play correctly without getting in the way of the action.

Examples: Typical umpire positions

the cone

Stay out of the way: The second base umpire will often position himself behind second base but outside of the batter's line of vision to keep from distracting him. This area is known as "the cone." It also gives the umpire a clear view of the pitcher. If the batter is left-handed, the umpire will stay on the right side of the cone. If the batter is right handed, the umpire will shift to the left side of the cone.

Move to the best spot to see the play: If there is a runner on first base, the first base umpire will move closer to first base, and the umpire that was behind second will shift below second base. This will provide each of them with a better view of the action.

Instructions to the Umpires

Overview: Once they have entered the field, umpires are instructed to follow a strict code of conduct. While the players and other team members are certainly part of baseball, the rules below ensure that umpires proudly represent the sport.

Umpires are given instructions in addition to the one requiring them to be in the best position to see a play. These additional instructions can be divided into things umpires *must* do, things umpires *must not* do, and things umpires should *avoid*.

An umpire *must*

- remember that making a correct call is his first responsibility, more important than *umpire dignity*. (Conveniently, the term *umpire dignity* is not defined.)
- remain active and alert.
- keep the game going.
- keep his eye on the ball, even at the expense of missing other action on the field. The instructions state that it is more important to know the status of the ball than to see whether or not a runner missed touching a base.
- after calling a player out, watch for dropped balls.
- keep his uniform in proper condition.
- remain courteous to officers of the teams.
- be patient, use good judgment, maintain self-control, and not lose his temper.

- treat each team equally, not judge plays differently for the visiting or home team.
- be courteous, impartial, and firm. By doing so, umpires will gain respect.
- develop a set of simple signals with the other umpires to indicate when an incorrect call has been made, so that the erroneous call can be corrected.
- carry a rule book. Umpires are encouraged to consult the rule book when necessary, even if it delays the game. The point is that it is better to delay the game to confirm that a ruling is correct, than to have the game protested later, possibly requiring a replay of the game.

An umpire *must not*

- hold conversations with the players.
- enter the coaching box or hold a conversation with the coach.
- make calls too rapidly, or turn away from the action too soon when a fielder throws the ball in an attempt at a double-play.

- begin to signal "safe" or "out" until the play at that base is complete.
- "compensate" for a bad call, if one is made, by trying to "even up" later in the game. Each call on a play must be made as it is seen.
- be fazed by criticism about a call.

On that last point:

If sure about a call, an umpire should not be intimidated by players' appeals to ask for second opinions from other umpires.

If not sure about a call, an umpire must consult with other umpires. However, he should not over rely on this measure. His first responsibility is to call the play correctly. He should request assistance from other umpires only when help is required to ensure a correct call.

Umpires must *avoid*

The official rules call for the umpires to "avoid" two things: visiting a team's offices, and "thoughtless familiarity" with a team's staff.

The Umpire-in-Chief and the Field Umpires

Overview: The rules call for one or more umpires to be appointed by the league president to officiate at each game. Four umpires are standard practice at a game. Any number over one, of course, sets up the possibility of disagreement between umpires. Here is how the rules handle it.

Games with only one umpire

If there is only one umpire officiating at a game, he takes complete responsibility for administering the rules.

While he will usually take a position behind the catcher, he is allowed to take any position on the field that will provide him with the best vantage point. For instance, if there are runners on base, he may elect to stand behind the pitcher.

Games with two or more umpires

When two or more umpires are assigned to a game, one umpire will be appointed umpire-in-chief. The other umpires become field umpires. A field umpire's authority equals that of the umpire-in-chief, with the exception of game forfeits, terminating a game, and a few other calls — those can only be called by the umpire-in-chief.

That said, the umpire-in-chief and the field umpires work as a team and have specific responsibilities delegated to them.

Umpire-in-chief

The umpire-in-chief is also called the plate umpire, since he stands behind the plate. The umpire-in-chief's responsibilities include:

- ultimate responsibility for the game's conduct.

- passing the batting order to the official scorer, including any changes.

- calling pitches as either balls or strikes.

- decisions concerning the batter.

- decisions concerning forfeits of the game (a forfeit ends the game, giving one team an automatic win).

- announcing time limits before the start of the game (if any have been established).

- announcing any special ground rules he deems appropriate.

Field umpires

Field umpires may position themselves anywhere on the field. They choose their positions according to where they believe they will have the best vantage point for upcoming plays. Typically this means that in addition to the umpire-in-chief, one umpire each will be positioned at first, second and third bases. A field umpire's job is to assist the umpire-in-chief, since it is often impossible for a single umpire to simultaneously monitor every action taking place on the field.

Field umpires are usually in the best location to rule on plays made at the bases — therefore they typically make these calls. However, any umpire can make a call, and field umpires share authority equally with the umpire-in-chief in making calls on plays at the bases.

Responsibilities shared between the umpire-in-chief and the field umpires

The following responsibilities are shared between all umpires:

- calling foul or fair balls,

- decisions concerning the rules of the game,

- enforcement of the rules of baseball, including those regarding conduct and discipline,

- calling "time," balks, illegal pitches, and ball tampering.

| The Umpire | Umpires' Responsibilities Before the Game |

Umpires have responsibilities before the game begins:

- **Identify the managers.** Although typically not an issue, the rules require that, at least thirty minutes prior to the game's scheduled start time, each team identify their manager to either the league president or to the umpire-in-chief.

- **Check the equipment.** The umpire must make sure the bats, uniforms, and all other equipment meet the requirements of the rules.

- **Get the baseballs ready.** The home team is responsible for supplying the umpire with baseballs for the game. The baseballs need to meet the requirements for size, weight, and construction (see page 38). The balls are delivered to the umpire in sealed packages that contain the signature of the president of the league. The umpire is responsible for breaking the seal and for inspecting each ball. He then "prepares" the balls, removing the shine on the ball by rubbing each ball with a special mud.

- **Spare baseballs.** The umpire must make sure that the home team has at least one dozen extra regulation baseballs on hand, in case their use is required.

- **Keep two baseballs in his possession.** In addition to the ball that is put into play, the umpire holds onto two alternate baseballs, to place into the game when needed.

- **Check the playing field.** Check that all lines are clearly marked with chalk, lime, or other white material.

See the chapter "Before the Game Starts" on page 28 for more information.

Rosin bag

Umpires are required to carry a rosin bag. At the beginning of play, the umpire-in-chief will place one rosin bag behind the pitcher's plate for the pitcher's use — to be sure that the pitcher's rosin bag indeed only contains rosin, not other foreign substances. The pitcher can only apply the rosin directly onto his hands — not his glove or other parts of his uniform. Balls hitting the bag remain in play.

In poor weather the umpire may ask the pitcher to keep the rosin bag in his pocket.

| The Umpire | Disagreements Among Umpires |

When umpires make simultaneous, conflicting calls

While no umpire may question or criticize another umpire's decision (unless specifically asked by that umpire for assistance), situations may arise where two umpires make conflicting calls simultaneously. When this occurs, the umpire-in-chief will immediately call the umpires together for a conference (players and managers will not take part). The umpire-in-chief will determine which call will be upheld, basing that decision on the opinion of the umpire most likely to have had the best view of the play — therefore the umpire most likely to be correct. The play will continue based on this final decision.

As an alternative, the rules stipulate that the league president may designate an umpire other then the umpire-in-chief to take responsibility in making this determination.

| **The Umpire** | # Putting the Ball into Play |

Beginning the game

The umpire (or umpires) will enter the field five minutes prior to the start of the game, proceeding to home plate, where:

- the home team's manager hands two identical copies of the home team's batting order to the umpire-in-chief.

- on receiving the home team's batting order, the home team's manager transfers authority of the field to the umpire-in-chief.

  This means, in part, that the umpire-in-chief now has the authority to suspend or postpone a game due to poor weather or unfit conditions of the field, and determines when and if a game will be resumed.

- the visiting team's manager hands two identical copies of the visiting team's batting order to the umpire.

- the umpire checks the lists to make sure they are identical, and looks for obvious mistakes.

- on delivering the lists to the umpire the batting order is established for the entire game, and changes in the batting order, through substitutions for instance, can only be made as provided the rules (see page 161).

- upon confirming that the lists are identical and with no mistakes detected, the umpire retains one copy of each list and hands the opposing team's list to each manager.

Double-headers and beginning the second game

The second game of a double-header will start twenty minutes after the conclusion of the first game. The umpire-in-chief acts as the timekeeper. He may extend this interval to thirty minutes, but must notify both managers about the time extension at the end of game one.

Exception: If there is a special event scheduled to take place between two games of a double-header, the interval may be extended. This must be approved in advance by the league president. The umpire-in-chief must notify both managers of the effect the special event will have on the the start time of the second game.

The umpire-in-chief must start the second game as long as weather, time restrictions, and field conditions make starting the game possible.

In cases in which the first game of a double-header is delayed, the first game played that day will be considered the first game of the double-header, regardless of that game's actual start time.

However, if a game from a previous day was rescheduled, creating a double-header, the first game played that day will be the regularly scheduled game, and the rescheduled game will become the second game of the double-header.

Note: Mistakes in the batting order. While the list handed to the umpire establishes the batting order for the game, the teams are not bound by obvious unintentional errors or omissions in the list. For instance, if the list contains only eight names instead of nine, or if it lists two players with the same name without identifying which player was intended, the error should simply be corrected. The teams' managers or captains should be notified of the error and the team will be allowed to correct it prior to the start of the game.

Putting the ball in play

The umpire-in-chief (also called the *plate umpire*) starts the game by calling "play."

Throughout the game, whenever a ball is dead, play resumes with the call of "play" by the plate umpire.

If a foul ball is not caught, the ball is dead. The umpire must wait until all runners have retouched their bases before putting the ball back in play.

In any case, the umpire should only call "play"

when the pitcher, with the ball in his possession, has assumed his position at the pitcher's plate. The catcher must be in position and the seven other fielders are required to be on the field, in fair territory, when the ball is put into play.

Putting new baseballs into play

The two spare baseballs held by the plate umpire will be put into play when:

• a ball is batted out of the field.

• the current ball is no longer suitable for use (i.e., it has become discolored or damaged). See page 74.

• the pitcher asks that a new ball be put into play.

New balls are only put into the game after a play has ended and the current ball is dead. Even when a batter hits a home run, rules state that a new ball is not to be provided to the pitcher or the catcher until all runners and the batter have reached home. In other cases, it is provided when all runners have reached their awarded bases.

> **Note: Player substitutions**
>
> The umpire-in-chief, after receiving notice from a team, is responsible for announcing any substitute players.

Tools of the trade

Overview: The umpires have equipment to keep things running smoothly.

The plate umpire keeps home plate tidy — and clearly visible — with a hand brush like the one shown here.

Plate umpires can use an indicator to keep track of the strikes, balls, outs, and innings. In the major leagues, umpires can also use the scoreboards to keep track.

Suspended and Called (Terminated) Games

Overview: A called game will either be replayed in it's entirety, or ended prematurely with a final score. A suspended game will be completed either later that day or on another day.

Calling games due to weather or playing conditions

Before the start of the game, the home team's manager is responsible for determining if a game should be started or postponed because of bad weather or other unsuitable playing conditions (see page 188).

As soon as the game starts, the umpire-in-chief takes on this responsibility. He becomes the sole judge to determine:

- if and when a game should be suspended due to weather or other unfit playing conditions.
- if and when the game will be resumed.
- if and when the game shall be called (terminated) after the suspension.

The umpire's responsibility, according to the rules, is to try to complete the game if at all possible. His decision to eventually terminate the game is based on his judgment that weather or field conditions will not improve and there is no possibility of resuming play.

After calling a suspension, the umpire is required to wait at least thirty minutes before terminating a game. While thirty minutes is minimum, the suspension can last for any length of time, even several hours, as long as the umpire believes there is a chance to resume play.

Suspending a game

In the event of a game suspension, the umpire signals "time." He does this by raising both of his hands over his head. The ball is dead when the call is made.

On resumption of the game the umpire signals "play" and the next pitch can be made.

Suspended games and double-headers

Following the first game of a double-header, the umpire-in-chief of the first game determines if the second game should be started or postponed because of bad weather or other unsuitable playing conditions. The decision is not up to the home team's manager and not up to the umpire-in-chief of the second game.

Suspended games due to fitness of the field

The umpire-in-chief assumes command of the field's ground crew and ground crew assistants whenever a game is suspended because of the condition of the field. The umpire-in-chief's goal is to make the field suitable for play. An unfit field is considered a violation of the rules by the home team.

Penalty: If the cause of the violation is not corrected the umpire-in-chief will require the home team to forfeit the game to the visiting team.

See the Weather chapter, page 188, for more information.

Ground rules

Each ballpark has a set of ground rules specific to that field's unique features — for instance, if the ball hits the roof in a domed stadium. The official rules state that the home team's manager may provide other special rules to the umpire and to the visiting team's manager. These rules will go into effect if both teams agree. If not, the umpire will impose his own rules regarding special conditions on the field, balls that are batted or thrown into spectators on the field, and other possible unforeseen events. None of these special rules, of course, will be allowed if they conflict with the official rules of the game.

Calling Balls and Strikes

Overview: The game of baseball centers on the strike zone. While it is carefully defined in the rules, the strike zone is wide open to interpretation.

The landmarks used to define the actual strike area, in practice, are vague. Each plate umpire will therefore see it slightly differently. Unfair? Definitely. But this dependence on interpretation, and the inevitable arguments that ensue, are all part of the sport. Baseball wouldn't be the same without them.

The strike zone is defined and discussed in the chapters on pitching and batting. The important point, from the umpire's point of view, is that his call of "ball" or "strike" is the final word. (See pages 70 and 84-86 for more information.)

Balls and Strikes | Check Swings

Rulings on "check swings" (half-swings) by the batter

A check swing, also known as a "half-swing," is a partial swing by the batter that may or may not qualify as a swing. That means that if the pitcher delivers a pitch that is outside of the strike zone, and the batter only swings the bat halfway (without hitting the ball) his swing may or may not be considered a strike. It depends on the judgment of the plate umpire. In some cases, a team can appeal the umpire's call. The official rules state that:

- if on a half-swing the umpire calls a ball, an appeal *can* be made.
- if on a half-swing the umpire calls a strike, an appeal *cannot* be made.

The defensive team's manager, therefore, may elect to appeal the call of ball on a half-swing, in belief that the batter swung the bat far enough to be counted as a swing-and-a-miss (i.e., a strike). However, the rules specifically state that the manager's appeal may only be based on the fact that the plate umpire did not ask for the opinion of another umpire before making the call, not that the plate umpire's call was incorrect. On the appeal, a field umpire must respond — the umpire positioned at first base for a right-handed batter, and the umpire positioned at third base for a left-handed batter. If the field umpire determines the swing went far enough to qualify for a strike, the "ball" will be changed to a "strike."

Implications if the appeal on a check swing is granted

If the "ball" is now a "strike" the status of runners may change. Forced runners who were freely advancing may suddenly be at risk.

If they already reached their bases however, they may stay.

Example: With a runner on first and three balls in the count, the batter makes a check swing. The plate umpire calls a ball, walking the batter, and the runner from first starts walking (or running) to second on the awarded base. On appeal the call is changed to strike when the first base umpire says the swing went too far. The runner from first is now stealing second, and can be thrown out,

Therefore runners need to be on guard. If they are not touching a base, they are liable to be thrown out. The catcher must also be on guard for runners stealing bases while the appeal is made, since the ball remains in play.

Forfeits

Overview: A forfeit occurs when a game is prematurely ended by the umpire-in-chief due to a team's serious violation of the rules. The offending team automatically loses by a score of 9 to 0.

Forfeited games

For a serious rule violation, the umpire-in-chief may end a game before it is finished, or even before it starts, automatically imposing a score of 9 to 0.

When the umpire-in-chief calls a forfeit he is required within twenty-four hours to submit a written report to the league president. Failure to submit the report, however, does affect the forfeit.

See the Official Scorer chapter, page 203, for rules regarding how a forfeited game is officially recorded.

Nine reasons an umpire-in-chief can call a forfeit

The umpire-in-chief is solely responsible for calling a forfeit. A forfeit can be called if:

1. the field is determined to be unsuitable for play. If the ground crew is unable to fix the problem, the umpire-in-chief may rule that the home team lost the game to the visiting team by forfeit.

2. one or more people enter the field during the game, preventing play, and the field cannot be cleared within a "reasonable time" by police or security personnel. The umpire-in-chief may rule that the home team forfeit the game to the visiting team. He must, however, allow a minimum of fifteen minutes for the field to be cleared before making this call.

3. a team refuses to take their position on the field or to play the game, within five minutes from the time the umpire calls "play." A forfeit can be called, unless for some reason the umpire feels the delay could not be avoided.

4. a team attempts to either delay the game or shorten it.

5. a team refuses to continue playing, or following a suspension of play, delays the action by more that one minute after the call of "play."

6. following a warning, a team continues to violate the rules.

7. a team does not comply with a ruling to eject a player.

8. a team does not show up for the second game of a double-header within twenty minutes of the end of the first game (unless of course the interval time has been officially extended).

9. a team is unable, or refuses, to put nine players on the field.

Appeals and Protested Games

Overview: Umpires can be wrong. If a team manager disagrees with an umpire's ruling, he may appeal, requesting that a second umpire verify the decision. In extreme cases, if a wrongful decision affected the game's outcome, a manager can protest the entire game.

Appeals made on umpire's decisions (protesting a decision)

If a team manager believes an umpire made a decision that contradicts the official rules, he may appeal by asking that umpire to revise his decision. At this point the umpire who made the call may consult with another umpire on the field. However, this is the only means by which another umpire may become involved. Umpires are not permitted to involve themselves in other umpires' decisions unless the umpire who made the decision requests assistance.

If the issue is not resolved to the manager's satisfaction, and the manager believes the umpire did not adhere to the rules, the manager can protest the game.

Protested games

Either team can protest a game, charging that the umpire made a wrongful decision that was not in accordance with the official rules. A protest, however, cannot be made over "judgment calls." Judgment calls are solely the decision of the umpire. See the following page for a list of judgment calls.

The league president presides over protest decisions

To make a protest, the team making the complaint must speak up *immediately*. The protest must be made:

1. at the time of the play in question, and;

2. before a next pitch is thrown or a runner is put out.

If the call being protested occurs in the final play of the game, the team making the protest must file the complaint with the league office before noon the next day.

If the umpire's call, in the opinion of the league president, was incorrect had an affect on the outcome of the game, the league president may call for the game to be replayed.

Judgment Calls by an Umpire

Overview: The single most important thing to know about judgment calls is they cannot be argued. A judgment call by an umpire is final!

Certain decisions in the rule book are categorized as "judgment calls," or "judgment decisions." This means the decision is up to the umpire. *Judgment calls are final!* Team members, according to the rules anyway, are not permitted to object to the decision. Judgment decisions specifically indicated in the rules include:

1. The suitability of the baseballs being used in the game.

2. Weather. The umpire-in-chief determines if a game should continue due to poor weather or poor field conditions. Or, at the end of game one of a doubleheader, he determines if the second game should be started due to weather or field conditions. The umpire-in-chief also determines if and when a suspended game shall resume, or if it shall be terminated.

3. Forfeit. Whether or not a team should forfeit a game for failing to appear on the field or failing to start play within five minutes of the call of "play." (The umpire will not declare a forfeit if he feels the delay was unavoidable.)

4. Helmet violation. If a team member does not correct a helmet violation "within a reasonable amount of time."

Concerning the pitcher

5. Injured substitute pitcher. Whether or not a substitute pitcher, who replaced a pitcher during a batter's time at bat, is injured before the at-bat is completed, preventing him from pitching and requiring another replacement pitcher for that batter.

6. Whether a pitch is a strike or a ball.

7. Quick pitch. Whether the pitcher's quick movement to step on the pitcher's rubber and pitch qualifies as a quick pitch (an attempt to pitch before the batter is ready).

8. Ball tampering. Whether the pitcher spit on the ball or tampered with it in any manner.

9. When to issue a pitcher's first warning. If prior to the start of the game, or during the game, both teams received adequate official warning about pitches being thrown to hit a batter, pitchers can be ejected from the game on the first offense.

10. Hitting the batter. Whether the pitcher intentionally tried to hit the batter with a pitch.

11. Warmup pitches. If a substitute pitcher will be allowed to take more than eight warmup pitches.

Concerning the batter

12. Whether a batted ball is fair or foul.

13. Batter interferes with a fielder. Whether a batter who is running to first base, when more than halfway to first, stepped out of the baseline and interfered with a fielder or a throw to first base.

14. Which bases were reached when interference occurred. On a call of interference by the batter, the umpire will determine which bases were reached by the runners before the interference occurred.

15. Interference with the catcher. In a situation in which the batter swung the bat and hit the catcher, if the batter hit him intentionally.

16. Bat tampering. Whether or not a bat has been tampered with.

17. Thrown glove. In a situation where a fielder threw his glove, cap, or other article of clothing at a fly ball, deflecting its path, the umpire determines if the ball would have otherwise been batted out of the field.

18. Whether a batter intentionally interfered with the hit to prevent a double play. If a batter intentionally interfered with a batted ball or a ball that was being fielded, to thwart a double-play, the umpire will call out both the batter and the runner closest to home.

19. Whether a check swing qualifies as a full swing. A full swing would result in a strike.

20. Fair or foul. In cases where a batter hits a fly ball near the foul line, and a fielder touches (or catches) the ball before it hits the ground, whether that ball is considered fair or foul. This call depends on the ball's trajectory, not on whether the fielder himself is in fair or foul territory at the time he touched the ball. (If fair, the ball would remain in play. If foul, the ball would be dead.)

21. Tagging up. Whether or not a runner touched his base after a fly ball was caught. (A runner must be touching, or must retouch, his base after a fly ball is caught before attempting to reach the next base.)

22. Batter's use of rosin. If because of weather conditions a batter will be allowed to step out of the batter's box to use rosin or the pine tar rag to improve his grip on the bat.

23. Whether or not the batter interfered with a batted ball either by intentionally throwing his bat at it or dropping the bat in its path.

24. Whether or not a batter or runner intentionally interfered with a ball in play by throwing or dropping his helmet.

Concerning the runner

25. If a runner is safe or out on a force play or a tag.

26. Whether the member of the offensive team tried to get out of the way of the fielder in an Interference situation.

27. Whether a runner intentionally left the baseline and interfered with a fielder making a play on the ball.

28. The bases that were reached by runners, including the batter-runner, at the instant a wild throw was made.

29. The bases that would have been reached had an obstruction not occurred. After a call of obstruction (an act in which a fielder impedes the advance of a batter or runner) the umpire will nullify the effect of the obstruction by awarding bases he believes the runners would have reached.

30. Whether or not a runner has abandoned his base-running effort by walking toward the dugout or his position on the field.

31. If a runner not touching a base interfered with a fielder who was making a play on the ball.

32. If the runner on base intentionally interfered with a fielder who was making a play on the ball.

33. Whether a runner reached the spot that "would have been" occupied by the base when a base has broken away from its designated location.

34. Whether a runner intentionally interfered with either a batted ball, or a ball in play being thrown by a fielder, to thwart a double play. If yes, the umpire will call out both the runner and the batter-runner on this violation.

35. Whether the first base or third base coach physically touched a runner, assisting him in running.

36. Whether a runner intentionally kicked the ball after a fielder missed a play on a batted ball.

37. The bases that were legally reached by runners before an interference occurred.

Judgment Calls by an Umpire

continued

Concerning the fielder

38. On a call of obstruction, whether a fielder was "in the act of fielding the ball."

39. In cases of spectator interference, the bases that the batter and runners would have reached had the interference not occurred. These are the bases they will be awarded.

40. Whether the fielder held onto the ball long enough to be considered a catch in cases where a fielder drops a ball.

41. Whether or not a third out was made before a runner scored at home, meaning the run would not count. If the out was made after the runner scored, the run would count.

42. Whether the infield fly rule applies — specifically, before a fly ball that is hit into the infield lands, the umpire judges whether a fielder will be able to easily catch the ball.

Judgment Calls	Judgment Calls *Not* Made by an Umpire

Some judgments are made by the official scorer, not the umpires

While umpires uphold the rules, the official scorer makes decisions that affect record keeping. The official scorer's judgment decisions include:

1. Hit or error. If a batter's advance is due to a hit or an error.

2. Stolen base. Whether a runner should be credited with a stolen base, or if he was safe only because of a fielding error.

3. Sacrifice or a base hit. Whether a bunt should be recorded as a sacrifice or a base hit.

4. Sacrifice fly. With runners on base and zero or one out, when a fly ball or line drive into the outfield is dropped by a fielder, whether or not the hit will be recorded as a sacrifice fly.

5. Error. If, and to which fielder, an error will be attributed.

6. Earned run. Whether or not an earned run will be scored.

7. Game won (the winning pitcher). In games where the starting pitcher does not qualify to be the winning pitcher, and there has been more than one substitute pitcher, which of the substitute pitchers will be credited with the "game won."

Note: To qualify as a winning pitcher the starting pitcher must have completed five or more innings, his team must have been in the lead when he was substituted, and his team must maintain the lead through the end of the game. See page 208 in the Official Scorer chapter for more on winning pitchers.

For more information on the official scorer's responsibilities in general, see the Official Scorer chapter beginning on page 196.

If an Umpire Gets in the Way

Overview: With four umpires on the field in a typical major league game, they are bound to get in the way from time to time.

If the plate umpire interferes with the catcher's throw

In this situation, the ball is dead, and runners must return to their bases. If, however, the catcher's throw is successful and a runner is put out, the umpire's interference will be ignored.

Umpires on the field

If a ball batted into fair territory touches an umpire:

- before it touches the pitcher or other fielder, or
- before it goes past a fielder (other than the pitcher),

the ball becomes dead and the batter will be awarded first base.

If a batted ball touches an umpire in the infield after bouncing over or getting past the pitcher, untouched, the ball becomes dead and the batter will be awarded first base (see page 117).

If a fly ball batted into fair territory passes a fielder, or deflects off of a fielder, then hits an umpire or runner, and is then caught by a fielder before touching the ground, it will not be considered a catch (meaning the batter will not be out on the catch). The ball remains in play.

If a pitch hits the plate umpire

If a pitch gets past the catcher and hits the plate umpire, the ball remains in play.

If the ball bounces off of the umpire and is caught by the catcher or a fielder before touching the ground, the batter is not out on the catch. The ball remains in play.

If the batter barely hits the ball, and it bounces off of the umpire and is caught by the catcher before hitting the ground, the ball is dead and the batter is not out.

If a pitch hits an umpire or catcher and becomes stuck in his mask or equipment, runners are awarded one base. The ball is dead.

If the batter barely hits the ball and it becomes stuck in the umpire's mask or equipment, the ball is dead and the batter is not out.

On the third strike

The third strike rule applies when, under either of the two conditions below, a pitch is missed by the catcher on the third strike:

- there is no runner on first base, or
- there is a runner on first and two outs.

This rule applies even when the missed ball touches the umpire. Under the third strike rule the batter becomes a runner and must attempt to advance to first base. This means the batter can be put out either by being tagged with the ball, or by a fielder with the ball in his possession tagging first base before the batter has reached it. See page 87 for more on the third strike rule.

If a pitch gets stuck on the third strike or fourth ball

The batter and all runners will be awarded one base when, on the third strike or fourth ball, a pitch gets stuck in the umpire's or catcher's mask or equipment (and therefore is out of play).

Umpire's Call of Obstruction

Overview: When a runner is obstructed, the umpire must decide the awards or penalties that will nullify the act of obstruction.

Explanation: It is up to the umpire to determine the bases awarded for obstruction. The intent is to award all the runners, including the batter, the bases that they would have reached had the obstruction not occurred. The actual number of bases is a judgment call by the umpire. The batter or runner who was obstructed will be awarded at least one base. Any runners forced to advance by the awarded base or bases would, of course, also advance. In addition, other runners may also be awarded bases if the umpire believes they would have otherwise reached those bases.

Calling "obstruction" and awarding bases

Umpires enforce the premise that runners have "right of way" to the base path. Obstruction is a violation committed when a fielder, without the ball in his possession and not in the act of fielding the ball, gets in the way of a runner within the baseline. This includes the catcher, who has no right to block a runner trying to score at home, unless he is in the act of fielding the ball or has the ball in his possession.

An umpire signals "obstruction" the same way he signals "time" — he raises both hands over his head. The ball is dead on the call.

Whether or not a fielder is "in act of fielding the ball" becomes a judgment call by the umpire. A fielder placing himself in position to catch a thrown ball can be considered to be in the act of fielding even if the ball is still in flight. If the fielder misses the catch, his "act of fielding" has ended and obstruction can be called if he gets in the way of a runner after missing the catch.

Example: A fielder who dives for a ball but misses, and ends up on the ground, blocking the baseline, must immediately attempt to get out of the way of any oncoming runners.

If there *is* a play being made on the runner when he is obstructed, or if the batter-runner is obstructed before he reaches first base the umpire will make the call immediately, At the very least, the obstructed runner will be awarded one base beyond the base he last reached before he was obstructed.

Note: When a wild throw is made during a play in which a runner or batter is obstructed, and an umpire calls "obstruction" while the throw is in flight, the wild throw rules will take precedence. This is to the advantage of the offensive team, since on a wild throw all runners will be awarded two bases beyond the last base they reached.

If there *is not* a play being made on the batter or runner at the time he is obstructed the umpire shall let the play proceed. He should only call "obstruction" when the play is complete. A putout will be ignored if it was made on the obstructed player before he reached the base he would have otherwise attained.

Penalty: As penalty for obstruction, the umpire will award bases to the batter and runners as he deems appropriate — awarding the bases he believes the batter and runners would have reached had the obstruction not occurred. If a batter or runner was put out before reaching the base he otherwise would have attained, the out will be ignored.

However, if the play is allowed to proceed to completion after the obstruction, if the obstructed runner continues to advance beyond the base that, in the umpire's opinion, he should be awarded, and he is put out, that out will stand.

Example 1: **Obstruction, immediate dead ball**

With a runner on first the batter hits a ground ball toward the shortstop. In a quick attempt to throw the ball to second the shortstop muffs the catch.

As he is picking it off the ground the second baseman blocks the runner's path. The umpire immediately signals "obstruction" and the ball is dead.

The obstructed runner is awarded second base. The batter, who had not reached first base at the time of the obstruction, is awarded first.

Example 2: **Wild throw**

The batter hits a ground ball to the shortstop, who has trouble fielding it. The shortstop picks up the ball and makes the throw.

As soon as the ball leaves the shortstop's hand the first baseman gets in the batter's way. The umpire signals obstruction, but the shortstop's throw goes wild into the dugout.

The batter will be awarded two bases on the wild throw, so he will advance to second base. The call of obstruction will be ignored.

Example 3: **Delayed dead ball**

With runners on first and second, the batter gets a hit to deep left field.

The runner coming from second is thrown out at home plate. At the same time, the runner coming from first is obstructed after passing second.

The umpire waits before making a call, because he wants to see if the obstruction affects the play.

The runner who was obstructed is tagged out while trying to reach third base, and the play ends.

After the play, the umpire calls obstruction and awards the runner third base on the assumption that he would have made it there safely if the obstruction had not occurred.

Ejections and Removals by Umpires

Overview: For really bad behavior, a player or other team member may be ejected from the game — banished to the club house.

Ejecting players, managers, and others from the game

Any umpire is authorized to disqualify a player, manager, coach, or other team member from further play in the game, and to eject the disqualified player from the field.

The umpire also has authority to eject other people, non-team members who may have permission to be on the field. This includes members of the ground crew, seating attendants, photographers, news crew, spectators, and others.

Eject vs. Remove

"Ejecting" and "removing" a team member are two options for the umpire specified in the official rule book. Technically, ejecting a player will ban him from the field, sending him to the locker room. Removing a player may simply send him to the dugout. Decades ago, removals were common, but in recent years, removals by umpires have come to mean the same as ejection.

Our discussion of ejections and removals in this section stays true to the official rules, differentiating between the terms. However, this is simply for nostalgic reasons. In practice, consider a removal to be the same as an ejection.

See the Misbehavior chapter, pages 178 and 179, for more on ejections and removals.

A thankless job

Umpires put up with a lot of grief during the normal course of their job. The scene below shows a typical day at the office for umpire Emmett Ashford, who is being verbally assaulted by Earl Weaver and Boog Powell during the 1970 World Series. As much as an angry player may resent it, the umpire has the final word. If things get really out of hand, umpires have every right to eject a team member.

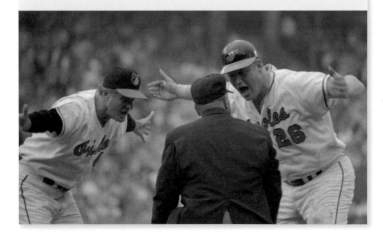

Ejections	Reasons for Ejections or Removals

Ejecting (or removing) a player

An umpire cannot eject or remove a player or other team member while a play is in progress. He must wait for the play's completion, then call "time."

The team member who is ejected must immediately leave the field and may no longer participate in the game. An ejected player must either confine himself to the clubhouse, or he may change out of his uniform and leave the ballpark. He may also sit in the stands, but far from the dugout or bullpen.

If a team fails to comply with an ejection (i.e., if the ejected team member does not leave the field) the umpire may call a forfeit of the game, giving the win to the other team.

Reasons an umpire may eject or remove someone include, but are not limited to, the following:

1. **Helmet violations.** This includes batters, catchers, and bat boys and girls.

2. **A batter uses a tampered bat,** an illegal attempt to improve his hitting. (The league president may impose additional penalties for this violation.)

3. **A pitcher has a "foreign substance" in his possession,** even if he did not use it to affect the ball.

4. **Non–team members.** An umpire may, if he feels it is warranted, eject anyone who has permission to be on the field. This includes members of the ground crew, seating attendants, photographers, news crew, spectators, and others.

5. **Unauthorized persons.** An umpire may eject anyone not authorized to be on the field.

6. **Fights and brawls.** An umpire may eject a player for assaulting someone or for being involved in any sort of physical altercation.

7. **Players, managers, or coaches leave their position to argue a call of ball or strike.** Leaving a fielding position, the coach's box, or the dugout to argue a call of ball or strike is prohibited. If the team member continues toward home plate after receiving a warning, the umpire may eject him.

8. **Unauthorized persons in the dugout.** During a game, only players (including substitutes), managers, coaches, trainers, and bat boys and girls may be in the dugout.

9. **First or third base coaches** who are either not in uniform, or who leave their coach's box position. See page 163.

10. **A team member tries to incite a demonstration,** attempting to rouse the spectators.

11. **A team member uses foul language** against a player, umpire, or spectator.

12. **A team member tries to cause the pitcher to balk** by calling "time" or employing other unsportsmanlike tactics.

13. **Physical contact with an umpire,** applying to any team member who intentionally makes contact.

14. **A fielder positions himself to block the batter's line of vision** or who otherwise attempts to distract the batter.

15. **A pitcher spits on the ball** after being warned for a first offense.

16. **A pitcher tampers with the ball** (see page 74).

17. **A pitcher delays the game** by throwing the ball to fielders other than the catcher.

18. **The manager makes a second visit to the pitcher's mound.** The pitcher will be removed when the manager visits him at the pitcher's mound twice in the same inning.

(continued...)

---

19. Second visit to the pitcher's mound, same batter. If a manager visits the pitcher's mound a second time while the same batter is at bat, after a warning by the umpire on his way to the mound, *both the manager and the pitcher* will be removed. If this takes place, the pitcher will complete that batter's turn at bat before leaving the field.

20. A pitcher throws the ball with the intention of hitting the batter. The umpire may also eject the manager when this offense occurs.

21. Intentionally damaging or discoloring the ball. The fielder who tampered with the ball, or, if he cannot be identified, the pitcher, will be removed (see page 74).

Note: The Official Rules of Major League Baseball can be daunting. It often uses different terms to mean the same thing. For ejection, it states a player should be "ejected" for the reasons numbered here as 1 through 7, "removed from the game and leave the playing field" for 8 through 14, "disqualified" for 15 and 16, "removed" for 17 through 19, "expelled" for 20 and "removed and suspended" for 21.

Ejections | Reporting Ejections

Umpires must report ejections to the league president

The umpire has specific responsibilities to the league president for reporting ejections from the game. At the conclusion of a game the umpire must report ejections:

• **within four hours**

  If the ejection concerned obscene or indecent language, or an assault on an umpire or any team member, the umpire must convey details of the circumstances surrounding the incident within four hours of the conclusion of the game.

• **within twelve hours**

  If the ejection occurred for reasons not mentioned above, or if the umpire feels that a rule violation or other incident that occurred during the game is "worthy of comment," the umpire must convey details of the incident within twelve hours of the conclusion of the game. This includes, but is not limited to, any other ejections of team members from the game (other than those that needed to be reported within four hours).

The league president may penalize the parties involved

The league president, after receiving the umpire's report describing ejections or other incidents, will:

• **penalize the team member(s).** The league president determines the appropriate penalty, which may include a fine, a suspension, or both.

• **notify the affected parties.** This means he will notify both the team member who is being penalized and the manager of that team about the penalty.

If a fine is involved, upon being notified, the team member has five days to pay. If he does not pay within five days he will not be allowed to play in any game, and not even be allowed sit on the bench with the other players on his team during a game, until the fine is paid.

The Umpire and the Pitcher

Overview: While there are many rules a pitcher must follow, here are some unsportsmanlike acts that the umpire must look for.

Ball tampering

Umpires need to be on the watch for ball tampering. These rules are in place to prevent the pitcher from altering the performance of the ball, which could unfairly work to the pitcher's advantage.

Before the game starts the umpire is responsible for inspecting the baseballs to be used in the game, checking to see that they meet Major League Baseball standards. He is also responsible for making sure the balls continue to meet those standards during play.

Additional details on ball tampering, including exceptions to specific rules, are covered in the Pitching chapter on page 74. As you can imagine when reading the list, these are judgment calls, and the umpire acts as the sole judge of whether or not these rules have been violated.

The umpire must not allow the pitcher to:

1. **apply any "foreign substance"** to the ball.

2. **spit on the ball**, or on his hand or glove.

3. **rub the ball using his glove, body, or clothing** (although he can rub the ball using his bare hands).

4. **deface the ball.**

5. **scuff the ball**, or use what the official rule book terms the "emery ball."

Penalty: The penalty for the above violations will be immediate ejection and a ten-day suspension.

6. **touch his mouth or lips** with his pitching hand while standing within the eighteen-foot diameter pitching circle (i.e., the pitcher's mound).

Penalty: As penalty for touching his mouth or lips, a "ball" may be called.

If the same pitcher repeats the violation during the game, the umpire may disqualify the pitcher, ejecting him from the game. The league president may also impose a fine for repeated violations.

Pitcher's behavior and possible ejection

The umpire is on special call to ensure fair play as well as the safety of the players. He therefore is required to take action against a pitcher who:

- **has a foreign substance in his possession.** The penalty for this violation is ejection from the game. The pitcher does not need to use the substance — just having possession of it is enough. For instance, an emery file in the pitcher's pocket can get him ejected.

- **deliberately delays the game** with the batter in position, by throwing the ball to fielders.

Penalty: On the first offense the umpire shall deliver a warning. For a repeated offense the umpire shall eject the pitcher from the game.

- **deliberately attempts to hit the batter.** This is a judgment call by the umpire, who may:

a. eject the pitcher, and possibly the manager as well, from the game, or

b. warn the pitcher and the manager, with the intent that the next such violation will result in the ejection of both of them. This warning may be issued before the start of the game or at any point during the game.

The league president may follow up with other penalties, such as imposing a fine or suspending a player from participating in upcoming games.

11 | The Manager and Coaches

A team includes one manager and many coaches. The manager directs the team and represents the team when dealing with umpires. First and third base coaches are required to be on the field during the game.

As with the players, the rules of baseball provide guidelines for the responsibilities and behavior of the team's managers and coaches.

The Manager and Coaches: contents

Basics for Managers and Coaches

Overview: A team will have one manager and many coaches. The manager is responsible for directing the team's actions. He also represents the team in ruling disputes, and often acts as spokesman to the press. In addition to a manager, two coaches are required by the rules — a first base coach and a third base coach. Other coaches may also be employed. The manager's and coaches' responsibilities, as they pertain to the rules, are discussed in this chapter.

Basics	Managing and Coaching Positions

Manager

Before every game each team must identify one person to act as its manager. In addition to directing the team and interacting with the umpires, the manager may also play in the game — although in practice this is the exception to the norm.

A manager may delegate some of his managing responsibilities to members of his coaching staff.

Required coaches

The rules require teams to position two coaches on the field:

- first base coach
- third base coach

Other coaching positions on the team's roster

In addition to the first and third base coaches, the coaching jobs listed below are typical. The actual coaching staff varies with each team — as do the coaches' specific titles:

- bench coach
- pitching coach
- hitting coach
- bullpen coach

First and third base coaches' boxes

Manager's and Coaches' Job Descriptions

Overview: The rules of baseball delegate specific responsibilities to the manager and the first and third base coaches.

Job Descriptions	The Manager's Job

The manager's job is to direct the team's actions and to speak for his team in communications with the umpire and with the opposing team. The manager must be identified to the umpire-in-chief or the league president by the team at least thirty minutes prior to the game's scheduled start time.

The manager is also accountable for his team's behavior and adherence to the rules. He is ultimately responsible for his team's recognition of the umpires' authority in the game — a point that is often tested when disagreements arise.

In addition to the responsibilities inferred from a coach's title, the manager may delegate portions of his specific managing responsibilities to a coach, making that coach accountable for certain aspects of his team's performance pertinent to the rules. The umpire will be notified of this beforehand, and from that point forward the actions of that coach relevant to his assigned responsibilities will be considered official — as if those actions came from the manager himself.

Substitute managers

In the event a manager must leave the field, he must name a coach or a player to act in his place. If he fails or refuses to designate a substitute manager, the umpire has the right to assign the responsibilities to a team member.

When a manager/player substitutes another player for himself

When another player enters the game as a substitute, taking over a manager's position on the field, the manager will continue to serve in his role as manager. His "new" position on the field will be on the bench or in a coach's box.

Job Descriptions	The Coaches' Jobs

Teams typically have between five and seven coaches on their roster. Most teams will include the following six coaches, although their actual titles are not limited to the exact titles shown:

The first base coach directs runners at first.

The third base coach directs runners at third.

The bench coach assists the manager in the dugout.

The pitching coach works with pitchers to improve their performance.

The hitting coach works with players to improve batting.

The bullpen coach works with the relief pitchers warming up in the bullpen.

Base coaches

A base coach's job is to direct the runners — instructing them to advance, continue advancing, hold up at the base or take other actions in their quest to score.

The rule book calls for two base coaches to be appointed per game. When their team is at bat the base coaches take their positions in the coach's boxes at first base and third base. Each base coach is required to wear the team's uniform and, with exceptions, must restrict himself to the coach's box during play.

Before the Game

Overview: Before the game begins the home team's manager is in charge of the field.

Before the game begins, the home team's manager, not the umpire-in-chief, is in charge of the field. He is the sole judge determining if weather or other field conditions warrant postponement of the game.

Exception: In the final weeks of the season, the league president may assume this responsibility — for concern that the manager's decision could potentially be influenced by factors other than the weather. The visiting team may appeal to have this shift in responsibility enacted.

Once the game begins, and between games of a double-header, the umpire-in-chief takes charge, determining if weather or field conditions will permit a game to begin on time. Between games of a double-header, the umpire-in-chief of the first game remains in charge of this decision for the second game.

Before the start of the game, the home team's manager may propose to the umpire-in-chief any special ground rules concerning spectators on the field, covering, for instance, cases where a batted or thrown ball may go into a crowd that has overflowed onto the field. If accepted by the opposing team's manager, these rules will be in effect. If not, the umpire-in-chief becomes responsible for creating and enforcing any special rules he deems necessary. None of these rules can contradict the official rules of baseball.

The batting order

Five minutes prior to the start of the game, the umpires and the managers of both teams meet at home base to do the following:

- the home team's manager hands two identical copies of the home team's batting order to the umpire-in-chief.

- the visiting team's manager hands two identical copies of the visiting team's batting order to the umpire-in-chief.

- after the umpire-in-chief confirms that each team's copies are, in fact, identical and contain no mistakes, he hands to each manager the opposing team's duplicate copy of the batting order. The umpire-in-chief retains the other copy for himself.

See page 34 of the chapter Before the Game Starts for more details.

The Team Captain

The position of team captain is primarily an honorary title given to a player. Although he may have other responsibilities designated to him by his team, the team captain may simply lead his team onto the field. The position of captain is only mentioned once in the official rules of baseball: if the umpire-in-chief discovers an error in the batting order, he may inform either the team manager or the team captain.

Teams are under no obligation to appoint a captain.

Requesting a Time Out, and Substitutes

Overview: A manager may request a time out to replace a player with a substitute, or to speak with a player.

Manager's request for a "time out"

The manager can ask the umpire to call "time" when:

- the manager wishes to make a substitution.

- the manager wants to have a discussion with a player.

The umpire may also call "time" if he wants to speak with one or both managers.

Upon calling "time" the ball is dead and no runners may advance.

Substitute players and the batting order

The manager must inform the umpire when he substitutes a player. The new player will replace that player on the field, and will come to bat in that player's position in the batting order.

When more than one substitute player enters the game at the same time, the manager must specify which vacated position each substitute will take in the batting order. The umpire-in-chief, in turn, notifies the game's official scorer. If the manager does not provide this information, the umpire-in-chief may assign their batting order positions to the vacated spots.

Managers and Coaches | Base Coaches' Positions

Definition of "within the coach's box"

The official rule book provides guidelines for a first or third base coach's position within the coach's box — although in practice umpires are very lenient on these rules. According to the rule book, base coaches may be permitted to do the following:

- **Position one foot outside the coach's box.**

- **Position both feet outside, but near, the coach's box lines,** provided the opposing team's manager does not object. If there is an objection, the umpire will require base coaches on both teams to strictly stay within the lines.

- **Leave the coach's box.** If there is a play being made on a runner at the base coach's base, the base coach may be permitted to leave the coach's box to advise the runner — signaling him to continue on to the next base, slide, or return to a previous base. In doing so the base coach cannot, of course, touch the runner or physically interfere with the actual play. This is considered interference, and as a penalty the runner will be called out.

The Manager and the Pitcher

Overview: Among other things, the rules limit the number of times a manager can visit the pitcher during an inning.

Pitchers may take another position on the field.

A manager may move a pitcher to a different playing position and later that inning move him back to pitch again. If he does, he cannot move him again during that same inning.

The umpire may eject a manager when the pitcher throws to hit a batter.

Pitching to hit a batter is strictly prohibited. The umpire will eject the pitcher, and at his discretion may eject both the manager and the pitcher, when a pitcher deliberately throws a pitch to hit a batter.

On the first occurrence, the umpire may warn the managers and the pitchers of both teams. When warranted, the umpire may choose to issue this first warning prior to the start of the game, or at any point thereafter. This means the pitcher, and possibly the manager, may be ejected on the first pitch that, in the umpire's opinion, is intentionally aimed at the batter.

Manager's and coaches' visits to the pitcher's mound

"Visiting" the pitcher's mound means stepping within a circle eighteen feet in diameter centered on the pitcher's rubber — the size of the pitcher's mound.

The number of times a manager or coach can visit a pitcher is limited — in effect, to just once per inning. On a second visit the pitcher must be removed and a substitute must take his place. A "first visit" to the new pitcher is allowed in that same inning, although not while the same batter is still at bat.

Exceptions: Visits during the pitcher's warm-up time are not included in the count — the manager and coaches are free to visit the pitcher during his eight warm-up pitches or within his one-minute warm-up time limit. They are also free to visit the pitcher when an umpire calls "time" at the request of the opposing team. A visit under these circumstances will not be counted — as long as the visit ends with the time out.

With the same batter up, a manager may not visit that pitcher again in the same inning.

If, after being warned by the umpire, the manager makes a second visit to the mound, in the same inning with the same pitcher and the same batter, then:

- the manager will be removed from the game, and
- the pitcher, following that batter's turn at bat, will be removed from the game.

For more details on manager's and coach's visits to the pitcher's mound, see page 77 in the Pitching chapter.

The eighteen-foot diameter circle

Note that the pitcher's mound is eighteen feet in diameter — but the pitcher's plate is not directly in the center of the mound. The plate is located eighteen inches behind the center, towards second base. A "visit" by the coach or manager specifies an eighteen-foot circle centered on the pitcher's plate. This is almost, but not quite, the area described by the pitcher's mound.

Misbehavior by Managers and Coaches

Overview: Several rules pertain to the behavior of the managers and the first and third base coaches.

Managers' and coaches' behavior

A manger or coach (or any other team member in uniform) is not allowed to speak to or communicate with any of the spectators.

Managers, coaches, and other team members are also, according to the rules, not permitted to socialize with members of the opposing team, either prior to or during a game. The umpires are rather lax about the enforcement of this rule, however.

During their team's time at bat, base coaches are required to be in uniform and to remain in their coach's boxes.

Managers and coaches can be ejected from a game.

Managers and coaches can be ejected from the game and ordered to leave the playing field for the following reasons:

1. If they try to incite a demonstration by the spectators.

2. If they use foul language against a player, umpire, or spectator.

3. If they try to cause the pitcher to commit a balk — by calling "time" or through other tactics.

4. If they intentionally make physical contact with an umpire.

5. If the first or third base coaches are either not in uniform, or if they leave their coach's box position.

Note: Reasons 1 through 4 apply to all team members, not just managers and coaches.

A manager, coach, trainer, or other team member who is ejected from a game must vacate the field. He is no longer allowed to participate in the game. Failure to comply can result in his team forfeiting the game.

Upon exiting the field he must either confine himself to the clubhouse or change out of his uniform. If he chooses the latter, he must either leave the ballpark or he may sit in the stands far from the dugout or bullpen.

An ejection subjects the team member, at the discretion of the league president, to a suspension, a fine, or both. A suspended manager, coach, or other team member is prohibited from entering the dugout or a press box during a game.

See page 152 in the Umpires chapter for more on ejections and removals.

If a base coach is touched by a thrown ball or interferes with a thrown ball

- If a base coach is touched by a thrown ball, by accident, the ball remains in play.
- If the base coach deliberately interferes with a thrown ball, the ball will be dead and the batter or runner will be called out.

Interference by a base coach

There are two circumstances under which interference will be called on a base coach:

- If either the first or third base coach physically contacts a runner, helping him to advance, remain on, or return to a base.
- If, with a runner on third base, a base coach leaves his position in the coach's box or performs movements that attract a throw by a fielder.

Remaining in the coach's box

Umpires typically do not strictly enforce the rules requiring the first and third base coaches to remain in their boxes — although getting too close to the foul line is not allowed. For one thing, if too near the foul line coaches may be able to see the signals being given by the catcher to the pitcher.

Protested Games

A protest is an official complaint filed with a league president charging that an umpire made a decision that does not comply with the official rules of baseball — or that an umpire failed to make a crucial call.

Any call other than those considered "judgment calls" can be protested.

A manager from either team can protest a game, speaking for his team when the protest is made. He must make the protest *immediately*. This means:

1. at the time the play is made, or

2. before the next play, meaning before the next pitch is thrown or before a runner is put out on the next play.

If the call being protested occurs in the final play of the game, the manager making the protest must file the complaint with the league office before noon the next day.

Each league has the ability to establish its own procedures for handling protested games. If the league president determines the rule violation affected the outcome of the game, he may require that the game be replayed. On the rescheduled date the game may be restarted from the point the protested play took place, rather than replaying the entire game.

Rescheduling a game is, of course, a major decision and is a rare event. The league president will have the final word on this decision.

Note: Judgment calls cannot be protested. A judgment decision is completely up to the umpire and, although a team can appeal to that umpire by asking him to seek a second opinion from another umpire, a judgment call cannot be argued or officially contested — no matter how incorrect that call may seem.

Of course, in reality, players express their displeasure over umpires' calls, including judgment calls, all the time. But the umpires are protected by the rules.

For more information on protests and on judgment calls, see the Umpires chapter starting on page 134.

Rulings on check swings cannot be protested

An umpire's call of "ball" or "strike" is a judgment call. If a batter's check swing (a half-swing) is called a ball, the defense may appeal to obtain a second umpire's opinion. This final call cannot be protested. As a judgment call, the umpire's word is final. Also see pages 87 and 143.

Example of a protest

In a 1983 game between the Kansas City Royals and the New York Yankees, Yankee manager Billy Martin charged that George Brett's ninth-inning two-run home run for the Royals was made with an illegal bat. Pine tar was applied to the handle beyond the eighteen-inch limit. Brett was called out, and then ejected after expressing his feelings to the umpire. The Yankees won 4-3. The Royals protested, charging that the umpire's decision was not in accordance with the rules. The rules state that when a pine tar infraction is discovered the bat should simply be removed from the game. The league president upheld the protest and the game was replayed several weeks later, picking up after the completed home run play.

12 | Misbehavior

Clearing the dugout to brawl with members of the opposing team is against the rules. So is arguing with an umpire. Umpires are responsible for maintaining proper discipline and sportsmanlike conduct. The way this is handled in practice depends on the situation — and on the umpire.

The following pages explain what the rules say about various types of misconduct. In practice, each umpire will interpret these rules differently and will determine, individually, when someone has made the transition from sportsmanlike to unsportsmanlike behavior.

Misbehavior: contents

Misbehavior

Umpires are responsible for discipline on the field. Players are not allowed to fight or to be friendly with the opposing team, or with spectators.

page 168

Steroids and Other Drugs

Steroids and other drugs are not discussed in the official rules of baseball. They are dealt with in an agreement called the Major League Constitution.

page 169

Misbehavior and Interference

Interference typically, but not always, refers to an act by the offense that hinders a fielder making a play. The player's "intent" can make a difference.

page 170

Misbehaving in the Dugout

Runners, the batter, and even members of the offense in the dugout have responsibilities.

page 172

If the Pitcher Misbehaves

If caught tampering with the ball — by spitting on it, scuffing it, or discoloring it — it will be the last thing a pitcher does in the game before being ejected and fined.

page 172

If a Batter Misbehaves

Forbidden acts for a batter range from refusing to run to tampering with the bat. Some things depend on the circumstances. Hitting the catcher with the bat, in some situations, may be okay.

page 173

If a Runner Misbehaves

Runners can break the rules when they run outside of the baseline, or throw things at a batted ball.

page 176

If a Fielder Misbehaves

Unless a fielder is in possession the ball, obstructing a runner is forbidden. So is catching the ball with his cap.

page 176

Ejections

Severe infractions of discipline will cause a player, or other team member, to be ejected from the game — or to be removed, disqualified, or expelled.

page 178

Misbehavior

Overview: Team members must conduct themselves in a proper manner before and during a game. According to the rules, this means they can't be friendly.

Umpires are in charge of maintaining proper conduct during the game.

The umpires are responsible for maintaining proper conduct and discipline on the field during the game. They can impose penalties for what can be termed "unsportsmanlike conduct." Violations by team members can range from those that are almost indiscernible, such as ball tampering, to out-and-out brawls that can empty the dugouts. The pages in this chapter discuss rules that pertain to various aspects of behavior, or misbehavior, by a player or other team member. Rules regarding the behavior of spectators will be discussed in the next chapter.

In addition to enforcing rules specifically laid out in the official rules of baseball, umpires have the authority to make a ruling on any actions not covered by the rule book. An umpire may eject from the game any team member who acts in an unsportsmanlike manner through actions or language.

Team members may not interact with spectators or the opposing team.

Managers, coaches, or players dressed in a team uniform are not permitted to interact with spectators either before or during the game. This rule includes both friendly and unfriendly exchanges.

The official rules also prohibit team members in uniform from interacting with members of the opposing team — although in reality this commonly takes place. The rule specifically states that players of opposing teams shall not "fraternize" while in uniform. The dictionary defines "fraternize" as socializing with people with whom you "should not be friendly." Apparently, according to the official rules of baseball, this includes any member of the opposing team ranging from the manager to the bat boys and girls.

Players must carry their equipment off of the field.

At the end of each half-inning the defensive team's players are responsible for carrying all gloves and other equipment with them as they leave their field positions. They may not leave equipment lying in either fair or foul territory.

| Misbehavior | Bad Behavior That Can Lead to a Forfeit |

A team loses a game by forfeit when they:

- refuse to enter the field, or refuse to begin playing within five minutes of the call of "play" by the umpire.

- delay the game, or attempt to shorten the game.

- refuse at any point in the game to continue playing.

- following a suspension of the game (due to weather, field conditions, etc.) do not resume playing within one minute of the umpire's call of "play."

- after being warned by the umpire, continue to deliberately violate the rules of the game.

- do not comply with an umpire's order to remove a player.

- do not show up on the field for the second game of a double-header within twenty minutes of the conclusion of the first game (unless the interval between the two games has been officially extended).

- refuse or are not able to put nine players on the field.

Steroids and Other Drugs

Overview: Major League Baseball's policies covering steroid and other drug use are not covered in the official rule book. Drug policies are covered in the Major League Constitution, an agreement between Major League Baseball and the leagues.

The use of steroids and other illegal drugs is strictly prohibited in baseball. The Major League Constitution goes into great detail about drug testing procedures, and all players are subject to drug testing as outlined in that contract.

Players who test positive for drug use are placed on a "Clinical Track" to receive treatment. In addition, players face fines and suspensions that increase if subsequent tests also prove positive.

Refusal to take a drug test, or failure to show up for a drug test without good cause, is considered the same as a positive result.

In addition to steroids, other drugs specifically mentioned in the agreement include cocaine, LSD, marijuana, heroin, codeine, morphine, ecstasy, and PCP.

Drug use is a serious issue in baseball and the Major League Constitution will continually be updated to reflect an increasing focus on this problem.

Misbehavior and Interference

Overview: The term *interference* typically refers to an act by a member of the offensive team that hampers a fielder's attempt to make a play on a ball. The interference can be through physical contact with the ball or the fielder, or through acts meant to distract or otherwise hinder the fielder's attempt at making the play.

There are five types of interference:

The official rules of baseball discuss five different types of interference:

1. Offensive interference occurs when a member of the team at bat interferes in any way with a fielder making a play.

2. Umpire interference occurs in two cases:

- when an umpire hinders a catcher's throw to prevent a runner from stealing a base,

- when a ball batted into fair territory comes in contact with an umpire before going past a fielder.

3. Spectator interference occurs when a spectator enters the field or reaches from the stands into the field, touching a live ball or otherwise affecting a fielder's play on the ball.

4. Defensive interference, commonly called "catcher interference," occurs when any fielder, not just the catcher, interferes with a batter, hindering or preventing him from hitting a pitched ball.

5. Interference by others occurs when any other person, authorized or not to be on the field, hinders a fielder's play on the ball. This list includes photographers permitted by the home team, police and security personnel, spectators, and others. By being within the field boundaries they are all in a position to possibly interfere with a play.

Note: *Interference by others* is not an official baseball term. We are using it here to identify occurrences of interference identified in the rule book, but which do not fall into the other categories.

Interference vs. obstruction

"Interference" should not be confused with the call of "obstruction." Interference is an act that hinders a fielder's efforts to make a play. Obstruction refers to an act that hinders a runner's advance — a fielder blocking a runner on his way to the next base, for instance.

However, to confuse things somewhat, "defensive interference" can occur. The word *interference* in this case describes a fielder's act that hinders a batter.

Intentional vs. unintentional interference

The actions taken following a call of interference for an act committed by a member of the offensive team can depend on whether their interference was, in the umpire's opinion, intentional or unintentional. Upon making this judgment call the umpire will take the appropriate steps.

Intentional interference

Interference is considered intentional when a person deliberately performed the act. For instance, if a person other than a player catches a ball in play, it's intentional.

Touching a live ball can be intentional and innocent at the same time.

Example: A bat boy picks up a ball, unaware that the ball is still in play. Although it was an innocent act, the interference is still, for purposes of the rules, considered intentional.

When the umpire judges interference to be intentional, the ball is dead and the umpire may impose any penalties or actions that he feels will make up for the interference.

Unintentional interference

The interference is unintentional if the person involved made an honest attempt to avoid the interference. If he or she did, the interference is ignored and the ball remains in play.

Example: If a ball hits a person who tried to duck to avoid it, it's considered unintentional.

The penalty for interference is an out.

On a call of offensive interference, the batter or the runner will be called out.

Making room in the dugout

Members of the offensive team are required to clear away from any area needed by a fielder to field the ball. This includes the dugout. If a fly ball is headed for the offensive team's dugout, anyone in the dugout is required to get out of the way. Failure to do so will result in a call of interference, and the batter or runner on whom the fielder was making the play will be called out.

Rules are not in place requiring the defensive team to clear their dugout for a fielder. Because they will be helping their own teammate, their willingness to make way for the fielder is not an issue.

Misbehaving in the Dugout

The dugout

When not participating in the play at hand, players of both teams are required to remain in the dugout — which only players, managers, coaches, trainers, bat boys, and bat girls are permitted to occupy. If team members fail to remain in the dugout, the umpire will first issue a warning.

Penalty: On the second offense, failing to heed the first warning, the offending team member will be ejected from the field.

Players who are on the disabled list

The dugout is open to players on the disabled list. While the injured players may take part in pregame activities, during the game they may not participate in any activity — including things such as warming up a pitcher. While they can sit in the dugout, players on the disabled list are not permitted on any part of the field during the game.

Causing trouble from the sidelines

No member of a team — managers, coaches, players, substitute players, trainers, bat boys, or bat girls — may act in an unsportsmanlike manner, either from the bench or from any other part of the field.

Team members may not, or instance:

- attempt to stir up or provoke the spectators.

- use foul or obscene language against an opposing player, an umpire, or a spectator.

- try to cause the pitcher to commit a balk (for instance, by calling aloud "time" to trick the pitcher).

- physically make contact with an umpire.

- obstruct the batter's view, or otherwise try to distract the batter.

Penalty: As penalty, that team member will be removed from the field.

If team members in the dugout show "violent disapproval" of an umpire's decision, then after issuing a warning, the umpire has the right to order the team member or members to the clubhouse.

Optionally, if the act is such that the umpire cannot identify the specific team member or members responsible — for example, if an object is thrown onto the field from the dugout — the umpire may order all substitute players to the clubhouse. In this case a substitute will only reappear when he is called into the game by the manager.

If the Pitcher Misbehaves

A pitcher can misbehave in a number of ways, including trying to hit the batter with a pitch, delaying the game, and tampering with the ball.

Pitching to intentionally hit the batter

This act can result in an immediate ejection. (See page 170, and page 73 in the Pitching chapter.)

Pitchers must pitch within twenty seconds

Pitchers are responsible for keeping the game moving. When there is a runner or runners on base, the pitcher must pitch within twenty seconds of receiving the ball. If he fails to do so the umpire can call a "ball."

Ball tampering

A pitcher is not permitted to touch his mouth while he is on or near the pitcher's mound, apply any "foreign substance" to the ball, spit on the ball, his hand, or glove, rub the ball with anything other than his bare hands, deface the ball, or use spitballs or other variations that would improve his chances of striking out the batter.

If, after a warning from the umpire, the pitcher continues this behavior the umpire may eject the pitcher from the game.

Ball tampering by other players

The pitcher may receive the punishment if the ball has been tampered with by another player, if that player cannot be identified.

Ball tampering carries severe penalties

Ball tampering is considered a serious offense. The penalty for ball tampering will be immediate ejection from the game and an automatic ten-day suspension.

If a Batter Misbehaves

Batters must remain in the batter's box.

Once a batter has taken his position in the batter's box he may only leave if:

- the umpire grants the batter's request for a call of "time," or
- there is a delay in the game for any reason. This includes a delay by the pitcher.

When either of these occur the umpire will allow the batter to step outside of the box.

The batter may also briefly step outside of the batter's box between pitches, before the pitcher is in position.

Time may be granted to the batter when the pitcher is in the first stages of the pitching sequence. However, time will not be granted once a pitcher has left the set position or has started his windup. If a batter steps out of the batter's box at this point, the umpire will call "ball" or "strike" as appropriate — even though the batter is not in position.

If the batter hits the ball with one or both of his feet touching the ground but outside of the batter's box, the batter will be called out. The batter will also be called out if he steps outside the batter's box to swing at the ball when being intentionally walked by the pitcher.

Switch hitters cannot quickly change sides.

Some batters are switch hitters, able to bat right-handed or left-handed. If a batter switches sides when the pitcher is in position, he will be called out. Between pitches a batter is allowed to step between the two batter's boxes.

If the batter interferes with the catcher

Interference by the batter against the catcher depends on the batter's intent — or more specifically, the umpire's opinion as to whether the batter's act of interference was intentional.

For instance, if a batter steps outside the batter's box to interfere with a catcher who is fielding the

ball or throwing to a base, or if a batter interferes with a play at home base, interference will be called.

- the batter will be out
- the ball will be dead
- runners will return to the last base legally touched before the interference occurred.

Interference must have an effect.

Even if the batter's interference was intentional, if the catcher's fielding attempt or throw is successful and a runner is called out on the play (including a runner attempting to score at home plate), interference will not be called. The batter will not be out.

If the batter hits the catcher with his bat

If the batter's swing unintentionally interferes with the catcher (meaning, as long as the umpire believes the contact was unintentional) the swing is simply a strike. However, the ball will be dead, and runners cannot advance.

If a Batter Misbehaves

continued

For example:

- The batter's swing may come fully around and unintentionally hit the catcher.

- Before the catcher has a chance to catch the ball, the bat may swing fully around and contact the ball on the back swing.

In either of these two cases interference will not be called.

A batter must take his turn at bat.

A batter is penalized if he refuses to take his place in the batter's box. The umpire will instruct the pitcher to deliver his pitches, calling "strike" on each pitch regardless of the location of the pitch. The batter will be called out after the third strike even if the batter has not come to the batter's box at all. Before the third strike however, the batter may take his proper position in the batter's box. The strikes will remain in the count and the umpire will proceed to call balls and strikes on new pitches, as usual.

A batter must accept being "walked."

Rather than risk a base hit by a strong batter, a pitcher may intentionally walk a batter by pitching four balls far outside the strike zone, allowing the batter to freely advance to first base. A batter who refuses to advance to first base after being walked (possibly angry about being intentionally walked) will be called out.

The batter may not hit the ball with his bat a second time.

The rules regarding a hit ball being hit by the bat a second time depend on whether or not the batter's second hit was intentional.

Intentional: Batters are not allowed to hit a ball a second time. If for instance, the batter swings, partially hitting the ball and sending it straight up into the air, the batter may not hit that ball again.

Likewise, a batter cannot deliberately throw his bat or his helmet at a batted ball. If he does and the bat or the helmet makes contact with the ball in fair territory, and if in the eyes

of the umpire this was the batter's intent, the batter will be out, the ball will be dead and runners may not advance.

Unintentional: If, following a hit, a ball in fair territory comes in contact with the bat a second time, or contacts a helmet or another object, and if this second contact is judged by the umpire to be unintentional, the ball remains in play and no penalty is called.

For instance, interference will not be called, and the ball will remain in play, if:

- the batter drops the bat after hitting the ball and the bat inadvertently contacts the ball in fair territory,

- the bat breaks and the broken part of the bat comes in contact with the ball, a fielder, or a runner, in fair territory.

- a batted or thrown ball accidentally hits a helmet or other object lying in fair territory.

If the batter throws the entire bat into fair territory, intentionally or unintentionally, and it interferes with a fielder making a play, interference will be called.

Pine tar

A batter may apply pine tar to his bat to improve his grip — but it may not be applied more than eighteen inches past the end of the handle. If the eighteen-inch limit is exceeded however, it is not considered tampering. The bat will simply be removed from the game, and no other penalties against the batter will be imposed.

If the batter uses or attempts to use a tampered bat

Altering (tampering with) the bat can improve its performance — and is illegal. If a tampered bat is detected, before or after the ball is hit:

- the batter will be out,
- no runners will advance on the hit, and
- any runners who were put out on the play made with a tampered bat will remain out.

Bat tampering is a serious offense that will also cause the batter to be ejected from the game. Additionally the league president will impose a fine and a suspension.

Batter	Misbehavior On the Winning Run

It's not over till it's over

Players can sometimes get overexuberant on winning a game. They can sometimes even forget to complete the win. In an awarded base situation, for a run to score a runner must touch home plate and the batter must reach first — even though home base is an awarded base.

Exception: If, on the winning run, spectators mob the field before the batter has reached first base, or before the runner at third base has reached home, blocking their advance, the run will score as if both the batter and the runner had successfully reached their bases.

Example: The batter doesn't touch first, or the runner doesn't touch home plate.

With the bases loaded, the batter gets a walk. This forces in the winning run from third base.

In the excitement, the batter neglects to advance to first base, and/or the runner on third neglects to advance to the home plate.

The umpire will call the offending players out and continue with the game.

Note: This rule deals specifically with a game-winning situation and does not appear in reference to a normal inning. Presumably, the level of celebration necessary to forget to score would only occur during a game-winning play.

If a Runner Misbehaves

A runner will be called out if:

- to avoid being tagged out, he runs more than three feet away from the base line.

- after successfully reaching first base, he later gives up his attempt to advance to subsequent bases.

- after successfully reaching a base, he tries to confuse the fielders by running the bases in reverse order.

- when attempting to score at home base, he misses the base, does not attempt to touch it and starts walking towards the dugout (either because he believes he touched the base, or he is bluffing).

See page 105 in the Running chapter for more ways a runner can be put out.

A runner may not interfere with a batted ball.

If a runner drops or throws a helmet at a batted ball, making contact with the ball in fair territory, and the umpire judges the act to be intentional:

- the runner will be out

- the ball will be dead

- all other runners will return to the last base they legally reached before the interference occurred.

If a Fielder Misbehaves

Throwing things

A fielder at times may be tempted to throw things at the ball — his glove or other piece of equipment or clothing.

Throwing things at batted balls

A fielder is not allowed to throw his glove or other things at a batted ball, or to use an item "detached from its proper place on his person." For example, he may not use his cap to catch a ball. Penalties are imposed (bases are awarded) if these items make contact with the ball in fair territory — but not if the thrown item misses the ball.

Example: A batted ball is on its way over the center field fence for a home run. The fielder, unable to reach the ball and in a desperate attempt to prevent the home run, throws his glove at the ball. The glove hits the ball, and the ball falls in center field. The home run will be awarded and the batter and all runners will score at home.

If the fielder throws something at a batted ball that landed, or is about to land, in fair territory (a hit not destined to be a home run), and the item contacts the ball, the batter will be awarded three bases. This means the batter will advance to third base and all other runners will

freely advance to home to score. Because the ball will still be in play, after reaching third base the batter may elect to run from third to home, but if he does, he risks being put out.

The rules regarding thrown gloves and other items do not apply if the gloves or other items come loose accidentally, or become detached in the act of making a play.

Example: A fielder reaches to make a catch and his glove flies off his hand from the momentum, contacting the ball. The umpire believes the contact was unintentional, therefore the ball remains in play and no penalties will be imposed.

Throwing things at thrown balls

A fielder is likewise not allowed to throw his glove or other items at balls thrown by fielders. The penalties in this case call for two bases to be awarded to the runners and to the batter who made the hit on the play. As with items thrown at batted balls, no penalties will be imposed if the thrown item does not actually touch the ball.

Defensive interference: if the catcher or another fielder interferes with the batter

The batter may freely advance to first base when the catcher or another fielder interferes with his attempt to bat. However, if the batter gets the hit, reaches first base and all other runners advance at least one base, the interference will be ignored.

Note: If the catcher interferes with the batter before the pitch is delivered, the umpire will call "time." Interference will not be called.

The offensive team's manager can accept or decline the penalty.

The offensive team's manager can decide whether to accept a call of defensive interference or not. He may or may not consider the call to be to his team's advantage.

Example: The catcher interferes with the batter, the batter is put out, but a runner on second base advances to third base on the play. The manager is presented with two options:

1. he may elect to accept the call of defensive interference, leaving him with runners on first and second, or

2. he may reject the call of defensive interference, letting the out stand but putting a runner on third base, where he may have a better chance of scoring.

Fielders may not obstruct a runner

Runners have right-of-way when running within the baselines. A fielder who gets in his way will be charged with obstruction, unless he is actively fielding the ball, or he is in possession of the ball and is attempting to tag the runner out.

The rules differ depending on whether or not a play is being made on the obstructed runner.

If a play _is_ being made on the obstructed runner: On the call of obstruction the ball is dead immediately.

If a play _is not_ being made on the obstructed runner: If fielders were directing their attention to a play elsewhere on the field and there was no play being made on the obstructed runner, the play will continue to completion before obstruction is called.

In either case, the umpire will call "time" when calling obstruction, and will award the batter-runner and all runners the bases that, in his opinion, they would have reached if the obstruction had not occurred.

See pages 117 and 130 for more on obstruction.

Actions by a catcher or a fielder can result in the pitcher being charged with a balk.

The pitcher will be charged with a balk (awarding runners a base), the batter will be allowed to advance to first base, and the ball will be dead if:

- the catcher or a fielder comes in contact with the batter or his bat.

- the catcher or a fielder not in possession of the ball blocks a runner from third base who is attempting to score through a squeeze play or by stealing home.

Squeeze play: A squeeze play is a play in which, with a runner on third, the batter bunts in hopes that runner will score.

Ejections

Overview: The most severe penalty for misbehavior by a team member during a game is ejection.

An ejected team member must leave the field, and may face additional penalties — a fine as well as a suspension from participating in future games for a specified number of days. Following are a few of the ways a team member can misbehave. (For additional information see page 152.)

Reasons a pitcher may be ejected include:

- **ball tampering**

- **having any "foreign substance" in his possession** on the suspicion that he would be using it to his advantage to affect his throw or the ability of the batter to hit his pitch.

- **delaying the game by throwing the ball to other fielders** unless, of course, he is making a play on a runner. When the batter is in position, the pitcher is required to pitch. The first time he delays the game, the pitcher will receive a warning from the umpire. If it happens again, the umpire may remove the pitcher from the game.

- **pitching with the intention of hitting the batter.** This is a serious (and dangerous) violation of the rules that can result in the pitcher's immediate ejection, and possibly an ejection of the manager as well.

For more information see page 73 in the Pitching chapter, and pages 153 and 154 in the Umpire chapter.

Reasons other team members may be ejected include arguing balls, strikes, and other judgment calls.

The rules of baseball specify certain calls made by the umpire to be judgment calls. These decisions are solely up to the umpire. No team member is permitted to argue a judgment call.

The calls classified as judgment calls are listed on page 146.

The umpire's call of "ball" or "strike" is a judgment call. Therefore the batter, runners, fielders, manager, coaches, and other members of the team are strictly prohibited from leaving their positions on the field or on the bench to argue a call of "ball" or "strike." On first violation, the umpire may issue a warning. The second time, the umpire may eject that player from the game.

The same is true when a manager attempts to argue a ruling on a batter's check swing (half-swing), since arguing the call of a check swing is essentially arguing the call of ball or strike.

While a manager cannot argue a judgment call, he may, on any call by the umpire, make an "appeal." This means he can ask the umpire who made the call to ask for assistance from another umpire.

Of course, during a game, team members disagree with the umpires' calls continuously. It is up to the umpire to determine when the disagreement has gone too far.

Umpires shouldn't argue

An umpire is not permitted to criticize or argue a call made by another umpire. He may only advise that umpire if asked by that umpire for his opinion.

Brawls and outbursts

Serious violations of the rules of conduct may include anything from the use of obscene language to an out-and-out brawl. When violations of this magnitude occur the umpire is required to submit details of the incident (or incidents) to the league president.

In some cases, one short outburst may be enough for an umpire to immediately eject the player or team member.

Reporting violations after the game ends

Violations concerning rules of conduct that occurred during a game, including ejections of team members, must be reported by the umpire to the league president within twelve hours of the game's completion. The time limit for reporting bad behavior is reduced to four hours for blatant violations.

The league president may impose a fine on the team member and may also suspend that player or team member from participating in upcoming games. If a fine is imposed by the league president the team member must pay that fine within five days of receiving notice.

See page 154 for more information on umpires' responsibilities after the game.

Eject, remove, disqualify and expel

The Official Rules of Major League Baseball use four different terms regarding actions an umpire can take against a misbehaving team member: *eject, remove, disqualify* and *expel*. All four terms essentially refer to the same thing — ejecting the player or other team member from the game, and banning him from the field. That team member may also face a suspension and a fine.

In past years a "removal" by a umpire meant sending him to the dugout, no further penalties involved. However, few people can remember the last time this took place. Players and team members today are simply ejected.

(Don't confuse this however, with a manager's removal of a pitcher to put in a substitute. This is a different use of the word *removal*, and happens often.)

13 | **Spectators**

Of the handful of rules that pertain to spectators, two have caused significant confusion in the past and will continue to do so in the future: (1) fielders are allowed to reach into the stands to make a catch, and (2) spectators are under no obligation to get out of a fielder's way.

These and the other rules of baseball pertaining to spectators are discussed on the following pages.

Spectators: contents

Basics for Spectators

Spectators are an integral part of baseball — the game wouldn't be the same without them.

Spectator Interference

Spectators, at times, can get too close to the action. Other times, the action can get too close to the spectators.

Team Members and Spectators

Basically, interaction between members of the two groups is not allowed. Before or during the game, team members cannot socialize with the fans, or try to incite reactions.

Spectators on the Field

A number of rules are in place to handle situations in which spectators may find themselves on the field.

Basics for Spectators

Overview: Baseball would be nothing without its fans. Spectators are an integral part of the sport. They can influence a team's performance, affecting a players psyche through cheers or through uninhibited criticism. They sometimes can become a bit too involved in the game. This chapter covers the rules of baseball that pertain to the fans.

The rules of baseball provide specifications for the infield, the outfield, and the foul areas. There are no limits, however, on seating areas. In some stadiums fans may surround the players from every direction. Inevitably, they may on occasion get too close. Intentionally or unintentionally, mischievously or innocently, they may contact the ball or somehow hamper a fielder's attempt to field the ball.

Spectator Interference

Overview: Spectator interference occurs when a fan gets too close to the action, touching a ball in play or a fielder making a play on the ball anywhere on the field.

Spectator Interference

The issue of spectator interference can be extremely controversial. A spectator interferes with the play when he or she reaches into the playing field, or enters the playing field, touching a ball in play or otherwise interfering with the action. In some cases the umpire's call, laying blame on a spectator, will be obvious to all — but in cases where a fielder is reaching near or into the stands to catch the ball, and at the same time a fan sees that ball as a souvenir in flight,

controversy can arise. The question as to whether the fielder reached into the stands, or the spectator reached into the field to interfere with the play, can be a point of contention.

Unlike inhabitants of the offensive team's dugout, spectators are under no obligation to vacate their position in the stands to make room for a fielder making a play. That, matched with the prospect of returning home with a souvenir and a story, can lead to chaos. Therefore, while the rules are clearly written, actual circumstances can make things fuzzy.

Spectator interference is treated like interference by a member of the offensive team.

When spectator interference occurs:

- the ball is immediately dead,

- no runners may advance,

- the umpire imposes awards or penalties based on his opinion of what would have happened in the play had the interference not occurred.

The umpire may call an out (or outs), or may allow the batter and runners to freely advance to the bases that the umpire feels they would have reached had the interference not occurred. Or, he may call for a combination of outs and base awards.

Example: A spectator reaches into the playing field to try to catch a ball, and his action prevents a fielder from successfully catching the ball. The umpire will call the ball dead and the batter out. On the same play however, if there was a runner on third base and the umpire believes that he would have reached home, tagging up on third after the fielder's catch then running to home, then in addition to the out, the umpire will allow that runner to freely advance to home base to score.

If a fielder catches the ball in the stands

A ball is considered legally caught even if a fielder made the catch in the stands. Before or after catching the ball a fielder may reach, leap, or fall into the stands. As long as he hangs on to the ball the catch is still good. (See page 129.)

If the interference occurred in the stands

In cases where a ball is hit into the stands and hits or is touched by a spectator, even when the fielder is reaching into the stands to catch the ball, there will be no call of interference. The ball is already out of bounds. The hit is simply a foul or a home run, depending on where in the stands the ball landed.

If the fielder reaches, leaps, or falls into the stands and misses or drops the ball, for whatever reason, the ball is simply considered not caught. Interference does not apply.

If the ball bounces back onto the playing field

If a ball is hit into the stands, bounces off the seats or off of a spectator, and lands back onto the playing field, the hit is simply a foul, a home run, or a ground rule double, depending on where it first landed. When the ball bounces back it is no longer in play. The ball is dead when it crosses into foul territory.

Spectators | Spectator Interference with a Thrown Ball

If a thrown ball goes into the stands

If a thrown ball goes near or into the stands, the same situation can occur as if a hit ball goes into the stands — there is potential for spectator interference.

The same spectator interference rules will apply to thrown balls as hit balls. If interference is called, the ball is dead and bases or outs will be awarded.

If a thrown ball goes into the stands, interference is not called, even if a spectator prevents a fielder from making a catch. *Wild throw* rules apply. The batter and runners will be awarded two bases from the last base legally touched at the time the throw was made (the time the ball left the thrower's hand).

Team Members and Spectators

Players cannot socialize with spectators or with the opposing team.

While in uniform, before, during, or after a game, players, managers, and coaches are not permitted to interact with spectators. The rules specifically prohibit team members in uniform from sitting in the stands. (Team members in uniform are also not allowed to interact with members of the opposing team.)

Team members cannot incite spectators.

The rules prohibit any member of a team — from manager to bat boy — from communicating with spectators, vocally or through actions, to incite the crowd. This means a team member cannot act as a cheerleader, rousing his team's fans. Likewise, a team member cannot argue or use foul or abusive language against a spectator, and any physical contact is forbidden.

The penalty for violating any part of this rule will be ejection from the game.

Spectator interference — when to call security. Fans erupted at Wrigley Field during game six of the 2003 National League Championship Series between the Chicago Cubs and the Florida Marlins, when Cubs fan Steve Bartman grabbed for a foul ball being fielded by the Cubs' Moises Alou. Even though Alou would probably have made the catch had it not been for Bartman, no rule was broken. From many angles of view, the ball had crossed into the spectator area before Bartman touched it.

Angry Cubs fans expressed their feelings and Bartman needed to be escorted from the field by security for his own protection.

The following season, Cubs fans ceremoniously exploded the ball, blowing it to smithereens in hopes of breaking the curse that has kept them out of the World Series since 1945.

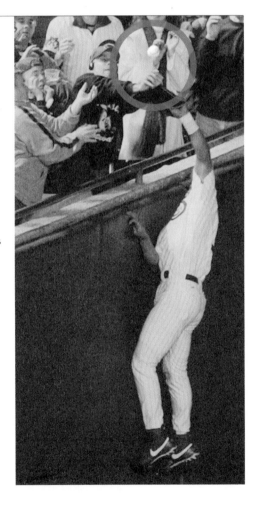

Spectators on the Field

Spectators are not permitted on the playing field.

The following people are allowed on the playing field during a game. They are not considered spectators. The people allowed on the field include:

- players and coaches in uniform
- managers
- umpires
- authorized photographers
- police and security personnel
- ground crew and other home-team employees

By special permission, spectators may be permitted to view the game from the field

The official rules of baseball allow for special ground rules to be established covering an overflow of spectators onto the field. Before the start of the game the home team's manager will propose special rules concerning balls that are batted or thrown into the spectators on the field. The visiting team's manager must agree to these rules. If not, the umpire-in-chief will determine any ground rules he believes are required, provided they are in accordance with the official rules.

If a spectator or a group of spectators enters the playing field

The home team is responsible for providing security and police protection during a game. If a single spectator or a group of spectators enters the field, the visiting team may suspend play. The home team will be given time — a minimum of fifteen minutes — to eject the spectators from the field.

The umpire will determine what is a "reasonable length of time" for clearing the spectators from the field. If the field cannot be cleared within this time, the home team will forfeit the game to the visiting team. Under the rules of forfeit in this situation, the visiting team will automatically win the game, with a score of 9 to 0 being assigned.

If spectators rush onto the field at the end of a game

Runs are not scored until the runner or runners have touched all bases, including home base. This is true even if a pitch results in a home run or a base-on-balls that will allow the team at bat to "automatically" win the game. Runs are not scored until home plate is touched.

An exception is made, however, if exuberant fans rush onto the field, blocking the batter's or the runner's advance. The umpire in this case will award the run or runs — a runner's inability to advance to home will be blamed on the spectators.

Interference rules differ for authorized individuals on the field and spectators.

The rules involving interference with people authorized to be on the field are different than the rules governing interference by spectators. The umpire's call in the first case depends on whether he believes the interference caused by the authorized person was intentional or unintentional. If ruled intentional, the ball is dead. If ruled unintentional, the ball remains alive and in play.

Interference with a spectator is never treated as "unintentional," regardless of the spectator's actual actions or intent at the time the incident took place. Interference will be called even if there was no malicious intent on the part of the spectator.

14 | Weather, Suspended and Terminated Games

The umpire's goal is to see that a game is completed. Sometimes this is not possible. This chapter discusses the effect of weather delays and the rules in place for suspending play, resuming play and terminating a game. In the process, it defines what exactly constitutes a "regulation game."

Weather, Suspended and Terminated Games:
contents

Weather, Suspended and Terminated Games

Overview: Factors such as rain or poor field conditions can affect a decision to begin the game, to delay play of a game in progress, or to end the game prematurely.

Before the game, the home team's manager is in charge.

Before the start of a game the home team's manager is in charge of the field. He decides if the game will start or be delayed due to weather or field conditions.

Once the game starts, the umpire-in-chief is in charge.

During the game the umpire-in-chief takes command from the home team's manager. More specifically, the authority is transferred to the umpire-in-chief as soon as the home team's manager hands him the batting order a few minutes before the start of the game.

The umpire-in-chief remains in charge throughout the game. From that point, among other responsibilities, he becomes the sole authority concerning decisions about:

- if and when weather, poor field conditions or other factors warrant that a game be suspended.

- if and when a suspended game is to be resumed.

- if and when a suspended game should be terminated (or "called") because resumption of play is not possible.

Certain rules exist to guide exactly when and where these decisions can be implemented. They are described in this chapter.

In games that may affect a team's standing in the league

Near the end of a season a game may significantly affect a team's championship standing. The league president may be asked to stand in for the home team's manager to decide, before the game begins and the umpire-in-chief takes control, if a game should be postponed due to weather or other factors. This prevents the home team's manager's decision from being biased — having his decision influenced by his team's chances of winning the game that day.

For example, if the home team has a star player on the injured list, it may be to the home team's advantage to postpone the game.

The visiting team can appeal directly to the league president (because at this point before the game, the umpire-in-chief is not yet in charge). If the appeal is granted, the league president takes charge of the decision concerning whether or not to reschedule the game.

The number of rain delays is not limited

The umpire's goal is to see that a game is completed if at all possible. This means calling multiple rain delays if necessary. As long as there is a chance that a game can be completed, the umpire-in-chief should extend the delay. His authority to order teams to suspend play or resume play due to weather or other factors is, according to the official rules, "absolute."

Weather	# Double-headers

In a double-header, the umpire-in-chief of the first game decides whether to start the second game.

If there is a double-header scheduled the umpire-in-chief of the first game, not the home team manager, will be in charge between the games, deciding if weather, field conditions or other factors will affect the start of the second game.

Delayed or rescheduled double-headers

If the first game of a double-header is delayed due to weather or other conditions, the first game played will be the first game originally scheduled for that day — even if that game would begin during a time that the second game would have been played.

If a double-header is taking place because an entire game needed to be rescheduled, the rescheduled game will be the second game played that day.

Minor League rules

While baseball games are typically nine innings long, the Minor League (also called the National Association) will allow its teams to play seven inning games on days when a double-header is scheduled. One or both games of a double header may be seven innings long. In these games, rules that typically apply to the ninth inning will apply to the seventh inning.

Weather	# Suspended vs. Terminated: Definitions

Once a game has started the umpire-in-chief becomes the sole judge for making the decision to suspend or terminate a game.

Suspend: A suspended game will be resumed after a delay, or if poor weather or other conditions seem unlikely to change, on another day.

The umpire-in-chief is the sole judge determining when play should be halted.

Resume play: The umpire-in-chief also decides when to continue play. A suspended game will resume from the point it was suspended. Runners, fielders, and the batter will all take the positions they held at the time of the suspension.

Terminate: A terminated game describes a game that has been prematurely ended by the umpire-in-chief. The game has been officially completed and play will not be resumed.

Terminating a game (a.k.a. "calling" a game) is a very last resort. The umpire-in-chief will only make this call when there is no chance of continuing play.

Understanding the fate of a game halted because of weather or other factors first requires an understanding of the concept of "regulation games." The definition of a regulation game, suspended and terminated games are discussed in detail on the following pages.

Regulation Games

Overview: A game must reach "regulation" status to be counted as a game in the eyes of the official scorer. Simply stated, to qualify as a regulation game at least half of a standard nine-inning game must be completed. The actual "halfway point," however, may be anywhere between the end of the first half and the end of the second half of the fifth inning. The rules ensure that, when needed, both teams have equal chances to bat.

Regulation games

When a game must be halted due to rain or other conditions, the decision as to whether to suspend or terminate a game depends on whether enough of the game has been played to qualify as a regulation game.

A game becomes a regulation game when:

- the fifth inning has been completed.

- the game is in the fifth inning, the visiting team has just completed their turn at bat, and the home team is ahead in the score.

- the game is in the second half of the fifth inning and the home team has just scored one or more runs to tie the game. It becomes a regulation game as soon as the home team's tying run scores.

A game becomes a "regulation game" in the fifth inning in one of three ways

To be considered a regulation game the visiting team must have completed their turn at bat in the fifth inning. Sometime between that point and the moment the home team completes their turn at bat in the fifth inning, the game will have become a regulation game.

VISITING TEAM   0 1 0 1 0
HOME TEAM   0 0 1 2 ⬤

The game becomes a regulation game sometime during the fifth inning.

1. If the home team is ahead the game becomes a regulation game as soon as the first half of the fifth inning ends (seen in the scoreboard above, where the home team is ahead 3 – 2).

However, if the score is tied when the first half of the fifth inning ends, it is not yet a regulation game.

2. If the visiting team is ahead and if the home team scores one or more runs in the bottom half of the fifth inning, to either tie the game or to take the lead, the game becomes a regulation game the instant the home team's runner crosses home plate to tie the score.

3. Any score: Regardless of the score, as soon as the second half of the fifth inning has been completed the game has become a regulation game.

Suspended and Terminated Games

Overview: When a game is called due to weather or other factors, that game will either be suspended or terminated. A suspended game will be resumed, either after a rain (or other) delay, or it may be rescheduled to continue play on another day. A terminated game will be ended — either declaring one team the winner, declaring a tie game, or declaring a "no game."

A terminated game will conclude in one of three ways:

One team will win: If a game has become a regulation game when it is terminated, the team with the most runs will be declared the winner.

Tie Game: A *tie game* is exactly what it sounds like. If a baseball game needs to be terminated, under certain circumstances (discussed below) the game will be declared a tie.

No Game: A *no game* is a game that has been started but has not yet advanced to be considered a regulation game. A *no game* will be rescheduled for another day, and will be replayed in it's entirety.

Suspended and Terminated	Major vs. Minor League Rules

Major League rules:

Tie game: If the score is tied when a regulation game is terminated, the umpire will declare it a *tie game*. The game will end in a tie score.

No Game: If the game is terminated before it has become a regulation game, the umpire will declare it to be a *no game*. The game will be replayed in its entirety on a later date.

Any score: With any score, tied or not, if a game is stopped *before or after* it has become a regulation game, the game will be suspended, not terminated.

Minor League rules:

Play will resume on another day, picking up where it left off.

If the suspended game is rescheduled to be played prior to another regularly scheduled game:

In the Minor Leagues, if play was stopped *before* it became a regulation game, the regularly scheduled game that day will become a seven inning game.

If play was stopped *after* it became a regulation game, the regularly scheduled game that day will be a normal nine inning game.

Suspended Games

Overview: Although weather is typically the cause, a game may be suspended for several reasons. The umpire's job is to see that a game is completed on it's scheduled day, if at all possible. In any case, a suspended game must be completed.

A game can be suspended for the following reasons:

1. Weather conditions make further play impossible.

2. A time limit has been set for the game (which can be permissible under league rules).

3. A legal curfew is in effect.

4. Vital equipment has stopped working and is preventing play. (Equipment may be related to water removal, tarpaulin placement, or other equipment necessary for keeping the field in playable condition.)

5. "Darkness" prevents further play. Since all Major League stadiums are lit electrically, this rule is rather antiquated — unless of course there is a light failure.

A game will be suspended whenever light failure or other equipment failure makes further play impossible.

A game that must be stopped because of light failure or other major equipment failure in the stadium will be considered suspended regardless of how many innings of the game has been played. The game will eventually be completed.

Suspended games must be completed.

If a suspended game needs to be resumed on another day, the remaining innings will be played:

1. Immediately before the next scheduled game in the same stadium between the two teams.

2. If no single game between the two teams remains on the schedule, the suspended game will be completed immediately before the next scheduled double-header in the same stadium.

3. If the suspended game was the last game to be played between the two teams at that stadium, the above rules will apply to the visiting team's stadium.

4. If following the suspension of a game there are no more games in the season scheduled between the two teams, the game will be considered complete (terminated), not suspended. The score will be final.

When a suspended game is resumed

A suspended game resumes with the game picking up exactly where it was suspended, either later the same day or on another day. It is simply a continuation of the game.

The batting order and the team's lineup will be unchanged. However, any of the players may be replaced with new players, provided that the replacement player did not play in the game before the suspension occurred.

Team members who have just signed up with a team may play in the game when it resumes. This is the case even if, when they joined the team, they replaced a player who played in the game but was replaced before it was suspended.

Pitchers. If just before the game was suspended a substitute pitcher came to the mound, and he did not complete the half-inning or did not pitch to a batter who reached first base, that pitcher is not required to pitch when the game resumes. However, he will be considered to have been substituted, and he will not be permitted to pitch for the remainder of that game.

Suspended and Regulation Games

Suspended Games

A game can be suspended if it *has not* yet become a regulation game, regardless of the score

The game becomes a suspended game (not a terminated game) if:

- less than half the game (as previously defined) has been played — meaning, if the game has not yet become a regulation game.

Or, a game can be suspended if it *has* become a regulation game and the score is tied

The game becomes a suspended game if:

- the game has reached or passed a halfway point (to become a regulation game) and the score is tied.

Exception: If a suspension is declared on a game that is being played near the end of the season — either a championship game or during the playoffs — and the suspended game is the second-to-last game scheduled between those two teams, the game will be terminated (called) rather than suspended. This means that the remainder of the game does not need to be rescheduled, therefore the teams will not be required to play more than one game on the day of the last game of the season between them.

If a game is suspended before an inning has been completed

If an umpire needs to stop play while an inning is still underway — because for instance sudden, severe weather conditions, light failure, or other factors make completion of the inning impossible — under the following circumstances the umpire can only suspend the game, not terminate it.

The game will be suspended when either:

- the score is tied and the visiting team was the last team to score, or
- the visiting team has scored one or more runs and they are currently in the lead.

These rules simply ensure that the home team cannot lose the game unfairly — before they have had a chance to bat the same number of innings as the visiting team.

Note: These rules do not apply if the score is tied at 0 – 0. With a score of 0 – 0, a game that is stopped after it has become a regulation game can be terminated, ending in a tie.

New players

When a suspended game resumes, players who have just joined the team may enter the game. This means, theoretically, if a player is traded between the two teams before the rescheduled date, he could conceivably play on both sides in the same game.

Rain Checks

A rain check is a "new" ticket issued to a spectator when a game is cancelled or suspended because of weather or other factors. It allows the spectator entrance to the rescheduled game, or to some other future game.

The rule regarding rain checks must be important — because it is listed twice, verbatim, in different parts of the official rule book. The rules state that rain checks will not be issued if the game reached the fifth inning and has become a regulation game (see Regulation Games on page 190). Aside from the regulation game stipulation, specific rain check policies are up to the individual stadiums.

Typically, if a game needs to be cancelled and rescheduled, the original ticket becomes the ticket for the new game. If the game is suspended, the ticket stub can be used.

Darkness

Still in the official rule book is a regulation stating that a game can be suspended on account of "darkness." A game will be called for darkness "when a law prevents the lights from being turned on." Otherwise, the umpire-in-chief has the authority to order the lights on when he feels they are needed. Assuming there has been no major electrical malfunction, darkness is no longer a factor in the major leagues.

Electric lights:

Under much hoopla, lights were installed in Wrigley Field in Chicago in 1988, making it the last stadium in the major leagues to go electric. Night games could finally be scheduled, and darkness ceased being a concern in Chicago.

Field Conditions

Field conditions can also be responsible for suspended games. A wet or flooded field, for instance, can make it unsuitable for play. The umpire will direct the ground crew to rectify the situation. However, if it is not possible to solve the problem within a reasonable time, the game will be rescheduled.

Game delays are not included when reporting a game's time duration.

One of the many statistics recorded by the official scorer at the end of the game is the time it took to play the game. If the game was delayed due to weather, light failure, or other reasons, the delay time is not included. The official scorer's responsibility is to report the time spent actually playing the game.

Weather, Batting and Pitching

Weather conditions and batting

If weather conditions are affecting the batter's grip on the bat, the umpire may grant the batter permission to step out of the batter's box to apply rosin or pine tar to the bat's handle. Otherwise, unless "time" has been called or unless there is a pause in the action, once the batter steps into position in the batter's box he is not permitted step out.

A batter's request for "time" will not be granted for any reason, even for weather-related complaints, once a pitcher has started his windup or has come to the set position. This includes a batter's complaints about dust in his eyes, steamed glasses, or other problems.

Weather conditions and pitching

At the beginning of the game, the umpire-in-chief will place a rosin bag at the far side of the pitcher's rubber. If it is raining or if the field is wet, the umpire may direct the pitcher to keep the rosin bag in his pocket instead of on the ground. The pitcher may apply the rosin to one or both of his bare hands, but not to his glove or anywhere else.

In cold weather, a pitcher may be allowed to bring his hands up to his mouth to blow on them in order to warm them. Under normal conditions however, the pitcher is forbidden from bringing a hand in contact with his mouth — a rule imposed to prevent spitballs (see page 74 for rules regarding ball tampering).

Pine tar, rosin, and resin

Pine tar is a sticky, dark brown substance derived from pinewood. It is used by batters to improve grip. Pine tar is typically applied to a rag, and then rubbed onto the handle of the bat. Pine tar may not be applied more than eighteen inches from the bottom of the bat's handle.

In addition to pine tar, both "rosin" and "resin" are mentioned in the official rules of baseball. They refer to the same material. A resin is a sticky substance derived from any number of plants or trees. Rosin is a specific type of resin derived specifically from the sap or from the stumps of pine trees. Sports equipment manufacturers use the more specific term "rosin" when describing their products.

Rosin is used by the pitcher or batter to improve his grip on the ball or bat. It is lighter in color than pine tar, ranging from amber to brown, and is contained in a rosin bag. The pitcher or batter applies the rosin by rubbing the bag between his bare hands.

15 | The Official Scorer

An official scorer is required at every game, responsible for recording virtually everything that happens. The scorer's report is entered into the permanent record books of Major League Baseball. Each game will generate long lists of numbers and names.

The umpires are not the only officials making judgment calls. Once a call is made, the official scorer in many cases may need to interpret the call, determining which specific players will receive the credit, or the blame, for the action on the field. The scorer, however, has no authority over the game's action.

The Official Scorer: contents

Basics for the Scorer

Overview: Major League Baseball appoints an official scorer to every game. The scorer operates behind the scenes — or more accurately — in the press box. After an umpire makes a call it is often up to the official scorer to decide which player was officially responsible for the specific action or actions that took place. This decision will go into the permanent record.

The official scorer

The official scorer records many aspects of the game for Major League Baseball's official records. When an umpire makes a call, the scorer will determine which player will receive the credit, or the blame. This means that the umpires are not the only officials in a game making judgment decisions.

The official scorer is positioned in the press box because part of his (or her) responsibility is to communicate these judgment decisions to the press.

The official scorer is employed by Major League Baseball, and like an umpire, he or she is an official representative of the sport. The rules require team members to treat the scorer with respect and dignity. Any infraction of this aspect of the scorer's rights will be reported directly to the league president.

Note: The official rules still state that the scorer can communicate the decisions through a speaker system, or through the old-fashioned method of hand signals.

Example: Box scores and abbreviations

Hitters	AB	R	H	RBI	BB	SO	LOB	AVG
D Jeter SS	5	1	2	1	0	1	2	.308
A Rodriguez 3B	3	1	1	0	1	1	2	.319
J Giambi 1B	3	0	0	0	1	0	1	.272
M Bellhorn PR	0	1	0	0	0	0	0	.209
T Martinez 1B	0	0	0	0	0	0	0	.244
G Sheffield RF	3	1	1	4	0	0	1	.294
M Lawton RF	0	0	0	0	0	0	0	.130
H Matsui DH	4	0	0	0	0	0	1	.297
J Posada C	4	2	2	0	0	0	0	.265
R Cano 2B	4	1	3	2	0	0	0	.294
B Williams CF	4	1	1	0	0	0	3	.251
B Crosby LF	4	0	2	1	0	1	0	.292
Totals	**34**	**8**	**12**	**8**	**2**	**3**	**10**	

AB	= At Bat		**BB**	= Bases on Balls
R	= Runs		**SO**	= Sacrifice Outs
H	= Hits		**LOB**	= Left on Base
RBI	= Runs Batted In		**AVG**	= Batting Average

The Official Scorer's Report

Overview: The official scorer includes many records in his report. The next few pages provide quick lists of the statistics recorded for each player. The rest of the chapter goes into detail about these records. In addition to recording the game's final score and the winning and losing team, the official scorer's report contains performance records for each player.

Scorer's Report	Pitching Records

Number of occurrences: The pitcher's records will include the number of:

1. innings that he pitched, counted in fractions of one-third according to how many batters he put out (see the examples below).

2. batters to whom he pitched.

3. batters to whom he pitched who qualified for an at-bat: An at-bat" will *not* be charged if the batter:

- hits a sacrifice fly or a bunt (purposely putting himself out to advance another runner).

- is walked by the pitcher

- is hit by a pitch

- is awarded first base as the result of a call of interference or obstruction.

4. hits made by the batters.

5. runs that the pitcher allowed.

6. earned runs that the pitcher allowed.

7. pitches that were hit for a home run.

8. batters that made sacrifice hits.

9. batters that hit sacrifice flies.

10. total walks (bases on balls) that he pitched.

11. walks that were intentional.

12. batters hit by a pitch.

13. batters who were struck out.

14. wild pitches thrown.

15. balks charged to the pitcher.

Name of the pitcher: The names of the pitchers will be recorded for:

16. the winning pitcher.

17. the losing pitcher.

18. the starting pitcher and the pitcher in place at the end of the game.

19. the pitcher deserving credit for the save (see page 209 regarding saves by a relief pitcher).

Example: Innings pitched

Example 1: If a starting pitcher is replaced in the fourth inning after putting one batter out, he will be credited with pitching three and one-third innings. If the substitute pitcher completes that inning, but a third pitcher starts the fifth inning, the first substitute pitcher will be credited with two-thirds of an inning. If the third pitcher completes the nine inning game, he will be credited with having pitched five innings (innings five through nine).

Example 2: If the starting pitcher is replaced in the fourth inning, but was substituted before any batters were put out — even if one or more batters reached a base or if runs were scored in the fourth inning, that pitcher will be credited with having pitched three innings. The increments of one-third of an inning are counted every time a batter is put out.

Scorer's Report

Batting and Running Records

Number of occurrences. The batter's records will include the number of:

1. **at-bats:** the number of times he came to bat, (except as noted at the bottom of the page).

2. **sacrifice flies.**

3. **bunts.**

4. **walks:** the number of times he received a base-on-balls.

5. **the number of walks that were intentional,** when the pitcher deliberately pitched four balls for a base-on-balls, rather than risk a hit by that batter.

6. **times he was hit by a pitch.**

7. **times he was awarded first base as a result of a call of interference or obstruction.**

8. **hits resulting in the batter safely reaching base.**

9. **runs batted in (RBI).**

10. **hits by which he reached second base.**

11. **hits by which he reached third base.**

12. **home runs.**

13. **the total bases reached on hits:** one if he singled, two if he doubled, three if he tripled and four if he hit a home run.

Example: If in the batter's first two at-bats in a game, he reaches second base on a hit during his first at-bat and third base during his second at-bat, the total bases he reached so far during that game will be five.

14. **the number of times he was struck out.**

15. **the number of bases he stole during the game.**

16. **the number of times he reached home to score.**

17. **the number of runners who remained on base when an inning ended.** This number does not include runners who were put out or runners who scored. This number will include the batter himself, whose hit put out another runner for a third out, on the basis that the batter reached, or would have reached, first base.

Names. The names of batters and runners will be recorded for:

18. **batters who hit a grand slam,** hitting a home run with runners on first, second and third.

19. **batters who hit ground balls resulting in:**

• force double plays, in which two runners are forced to run and are both put out.

• reverse force double plays, where a force out exists for two runners but the trailing runner is put out first, removing the force on the runner

ahead of him. This requires the defense to tag the lead runner, not just tag the base.

20. **runners who were put out trying to steal a base.**

An "at-bat" will *not* be charged when:

• the batter hits a sacrifice fly or a bunt (putting himself out to advance another runner).

• the batter is walked by the pitcher.

• the batter is hit by a pitch.

• the batter is awarded first base as the result of a call of interference or obstruction.

This is because the number of "at-bats" are factored into a batter's batting average, and including sacrifice flies or bunts, walks, or awarded bases would unfairly affect that player's batting average.

Scorer's Report	Catching and Fielding Records

Number of occurrences. The catcher's and fielder's records will include:

1. the number of pitches missed by the catcher, known as "passed balls." These are pitches that he should have caught, but because he missed the catch, a runner or runners advanced or scored.

2. putouts, the number of times he put out a batter or runner.

3. assists.

4. errors.

5. double plays in which the fielder was involved.

6. triple plays in which the fielder was involved.

Names: The names of fielders will be included in the records for:

7. fielders who took part in either a double play or a triple play.

Scorer's Report	At the End of the Game

Numbers. At the end of the inning or game, the scorer will record:

1. the number of outs in the inning when the game was won. When a game is won by the home team in the second half of the last inning, their number of outs may be less than three.

2. the score at the end of each inning.

Names. The official records will also include:

3. the names of the umpires officiating at the game, listed in this order:

- the plate umpire
- the first base umpire
- the second base umpire
- the third base umpire

The time duration of the game

The official scorer's report includes the time it took to play the game. This number is the actual playing time. Suspensions for weather, light failure or other reasons are not included in the playing time.

Starting Players, Substitutions and Improper Batters

Overview: The official scorer's report will contain the names of the players on both teams, their field positions, and their positions in the batting order.

Players' batting order positions and their fielding positions

In the official scorer's report, players fielding positions will be their nominal positions. If, for instance, a second baseman positions himself far behind second base, putting four fielders in the outfield, for purposes of record-keeping his position will still be considered second base.

If a substitute batter or substitute runner enters the game, the official scorer will use a special symbol that will refer to a separate part of his records, describing what the substitute did in the game. To keep the written records consistent, the rules recommend that the scorer use lower case letters for substitute batters and numbers for substitute runners.

Example: the scorer may write something like "player [a] hit a double

for Williams in the fourth inning," or "player [2] ran for Anderson in the fifth inning."

If cases where a substitute is announced, but before he has a chance to enter the game he himself is substituted, then the official record will consider the second substitute as being a substitute for the first substitute, not as a substitute for the original player.

Example: Player [a] is announced as a substitute batter for Williams, but before player [a] even has a chance to enter the game, player [b] is announced as a substitute, taking the position held by [a] in the batting order. Player [b] is considered to be a substitute for player [a], not for Williams.

Attributing outs when a batter bats out of turn

Situation 1: If a batter bats out of turn, is put out, and the proper batter who missed his turn is called out for missing it:

- the proper batter is charged with an at-bat and an out.

- the fielder (or fielders) receive credit for the putout and any assists, the same as if the proper batter had batted.

Situation 2: If an improper batter becomes a runner and the proper batter who missed his turn is called out for missing it:

- the proper batter is charged with an at-bat.

- the catcher receives credit for a putout (even though he didn't play an active role).

- the improper batter's advance to a base doesn't count — the records ignore his improper time at bat.

Situation 3: If multiple batters bat out of turn:

- the batters continue batting, skipping the batter who missed his turn at bat.

- the records for the batter's missed turn at bat remain empty.

Notations for substitute batters and runners

In their written records, the rules specify that the scorers should use:

Lowercase letters (a, b, c, etc.) for substitute batters.
Numbers (1, 2, 3, etc.) for substitute runners.

Box Scores

A box score is simply a table of numbers. For each team the table lists the names of the players from that game down the left side column. Across from his name are shown his number of at-bats, base-on-balls received, sacrifice flies and bunts that he hit, and other statistics from the game (see page 198).

The box score records will be accurate when:

at-bats
bases-on-balls
sacrifice flies
sacrifice bunts
bases awarded by interference
bases awarded by obstruction

equal

runs
putouts
runners left on base

Called (Terminated) Games

If the game is called after it has become a regulation game (i.e., if more than half the game was played), all of the game's records up to that point will be entered into the official scorer's report. If the game is called and it ended in a tie, a winning or losing pitcher will not be identified.

Forfeits

If a game has become a regulation game, and is later ended because the umpire-in-chief called a forfeit, the records up to the point that the forfeit was called will be counted in the official scorer's report.

If the team that is declared the winner by forfeit is:

- ahead in the score at the time the forfeit is called, the winning and losing pitchers will be named as if the game had been called at that point.

- behind in the score or tied at the time the forfeit is called, winning and losing pitchers are not named.

If not a regulation game: If the forfeit is called before the game starts, or before it has become a regulation game, no records will be included in the official scorer's report. The report will only declare that the game was forfeited. In a forfeit a score of 9 to 0 is automatically applied.

Wild Pitches and Passed Balls

Wild pitches and passed balls are only recorded when they allow a runner or runners to advance.

A pitcher will be charged with a wild pitch when the pitch is so high, so low, or so wide that the catcher, with "ordinary effort" cannot catch or control the ball. However, if the pitch is judged to be controllable by the official scorer, the charge will be a passed ball (a missed catch) by the catcher. In either case, a runner or runners must advance for the charge to be recorded.

Note: A pitch that hits the ground before reaching home plate is not automatically charged as a wild pitch — unless it bounces in a way that makes it impossible for the catcher to handle, and one or more runners advance as a result.

Base-on-Balls (Walks)

Base-on-balls

A base-on-balls is commonly known as a "walk." It is an award of first base to the batter when a pitcher pitches four balls (a pitch outside of the strike zone on which the batter does not swing). The official scorer charges a base-on-balls to the pitcher.

If, when pitching the fourth ball, the pitch touches the batter, the official scorer will record a "hit batter."

Intentionally pitching a base-on-balls

As part of his strategy, a pitcher may intentionally walk a batter, rather than risk a base hit that could advance other runners or send them home. An intentional base-on-balls is indicated by the pitcher's last pitch. Regardless of what he threw previously, if the fourth ball is pitched way outside the strike zone, requiring the catcher to leave his catcher's box to make the catch, the official scorer will record an intentional base-on-balls.

Note: If the batter refuses to advance to first base after receiving four balls and being awarded the base, the umpire will call him out. In this case, a base-on-balls is not recorded. Rather, it qualifies as an at-bat.

Strikeouts

A strikeout can be charged in four ways:

1. A batter strikes out on a third strike when the pitch is caught by the catcher.

2. With zero or one out and a runner on first base, a batter will strike out even if the third strike is not caught.

3. When the *third strike rule* is in effect — when with no runner on first base, or a runner on first and two outs, the ball is not caught by the catcher, allowing the batter to become a runner. Even though the batter becomes a runner, the official scorer still records a strikeout.

4. When, on the third strike, a pitch is bunted foul (unless the bunt is hit into the air and the catcher or another fielder catches the ball for an out before it touches the ground).

Note: If a batter has two strikes against him when a substitute takes his place, and the strikeout is completed by the substitute, the first batter will be charged with a strikeout. Any other outcome of that time at bat, a base-on-balls for instance, will be attributed to the substitute batter.

Earned Runs

Earned runs

An earned run is a run attributable to a pitcher's performance, or lack thereof. It means that the offense "earned" the run off the pitcher (as opposed, for instance, to getting the run on an error). For the pitcher, fewer earned runs is better. To determine the number of earned runs, reconstruct the inning without fielding errors, catcher interference, or passed balls (pitches missed by the catcher).

An earned run *will* be counted when it was made possible by:

- a hit.
- a sacrifice bunt.
- a sacrifice fly.
- stolen bases.
- fielder's choice or putouts being made on another runner or runners.
- a base-on-balls (a walk).
- a batter hit by a pitch.
- a balk.
- a wild pitch, including a wild pitch on a third strike that allows a batter to run.

If catcher interference (defensive interference) is called, an earned run will be charged if the runner scored at home before the catcher interference award of first base was made.

A run will not be counted as an earned run if, somewhere along the way, the runner reached first base or advanced to any bases due to a fielding error.

An earned run *will not* be counted when it was made possible by:

- a run is scored by a runner who reached first base as the result of a call of interference or obstruction.
- a run is scored by a runner who reached first base as the result of a fielding error.
- a run is scored by a runner who could have been put out while running the bases, except for a fielding error.
- a run is scored by a runner whose time at bat was extended because a fielder missed catching a fly ball in foul territory (because without that fielding error, the batter would have been out).

- a run is scored by a runner who advanced one or more bases as the result of a fielding error, a passed ball, or interference or obstruction (provided the official scorer believes that the runner would not have otherwise advanced during the play).

The official scorer must make judgments about fielding errors.

Before counting or not counting an earned run, the official scorer must evaluate the effect that a fielding error had on a current or previous play. On plays in which fielders committed errors he must determine whether a runner would have advanced had the play been errorless. If he would have advanced anyway, his eventual crossing of home plate will count as an earned run. If he was only able to advance because of the fielding error, his run will not be included in the count of earned runs.

Give the pitcher the benefit of the doubt.

In determining the effect of a fielding error the official scorer is instructed to give the pitcher the "benefit of the doubt" — meaning, if any doubt exists, blame the runner's advance on the fielding error, not on the pitcher. If that runner eventually reaches home plate to score, do not include his run in the count of earned runs.

Earned Runs | # Earned Runs and Substitute Pitchers

When a substitute pitcher enters the inning with runners on base, the number of earned runs already scored and the number of runners who are on base will determine the maximum number of earned runs that can be attributed to the first pitcher.

For instance, if the first pitcher puts runners on first and second bases, and is substituted, the next two runs to score in that inning will be included in the first pitcher's earned run count.

This number will be reduced if one or both of these runners are put out for reasons not associated with batting — for instance, if they were caught stealing a base, or if they were thrown out at a base (picked off) because they were not touching the base.

This number will not be reduced if their outs are associated with a batter's performance — for example, if they were forced out at a base, or tagged out while running the bases after a hit. Subsequent runs scored will be attributed to the first pitcher up to his maximum number — even if the runners who actually scored were put on base by the substitute pitcher.

Examples: **Earned runs applied to substitute pitchers**

Example 1: Pitcher 1 puts Adam on second base and Bill on first base. He is then substituted. Pitcher 2's pitch to Carl results in a home run. Pitcher 1 will be charged with 2 earned runs, while Pitcher 2 will be charged with 1 earned run.

Example 2: Pitcher 1 puts Adam on second base and Bill on first base. He is then substituted. Pitcher 2 pitches to Carl, who gets a single, but Adam is forced out at third base. The next pitch to Dennis results in a home run. Three runs score. Pitcher 1 will be charged with 2 earned runs, while Pitcher 2 will be charged with 1 earned run.

Example 3: Pitcher 1 puts Adam on second base and Bill on first base. He is then substituted. Adam is put out when he is caught stealing (an out *not* associated with batting). Pitcher 2 walks Carl. The next pitch to Dennis results in a home run. Three runs score. Pitcher 1 will be charged with 1 earned run, while Pitcher 2 will be charged with 2 earned runs.

Example 4: Pitcher 1 puts Adam on second base and Bill on first base. He is then substituted. Pitcher 2 pitches to Carl, who gets a single, but Adam is forced out at third base (this out *is* associated with batting). Pitcher 2 is substituted. Pitcher 3's next pitch to Dennis results in a home run. Three runs score. Pitcher 1 will be charged with 2 earned runs, Pitcher 2 will be charged with 1 earned run, Pitcher 3 will be charged with 0 earned runs.

| Earned Runs | Base-on-Balls (Walks) and Substitute Pitchers |

Substitute pitchers are not accountable for the first pitcher's count.

If a substitute pitcher relieves a pitcher while a batter is still at bat, the substitute pitcher will not be responsible for a walk (a base-on-balls) if the balance of balls and strikes in the count is in the batter's favor.

The first pitcher will be responsible for a walk if the count is:

* 2 balls and 0 strike
* 2 balls and 1 strike
* 3 balls and 0 strike
* 3 balls and 1 strike
* 3 balls and 2 strikes

In the case that the batter is eventually walked, that batter and the base-on-balls will be attributed to the first pitcher.

If the balance of balls to strikes in the count are in the pitcher's favor when the substitute pitcher comes in, that batter and his actions will be charged to the substitute pitcher.

The substitute pitcher will be responsible for a walk if the count is:

* 2 balls and 2 strikes
* 1 ball and 2 strikes
* 1 ball and 1 strike
* 1 ball and 0 strike
* 0 ball and 2 strikes
* 0 ball and 1 strikes

The substitute pitcher will be held responsible if the batter is walked. The substitute will be charged with the base-on-balls.

If that batter reaches first base for any other reason, for example, if he gets a hit or he is touched by a pitch, that batter's advance will be charged to the substitute pitcher.

Shutouts

A shutout is a game in which one team does not score any runs. A pitcher will be credited with a shutout when:

* he pitches the entire game

or, when the following conditions are met:

* he enters the game in the first inning, with no outs on the opposing team, and
* he pitches for the remainder of the game.

If two or more pitchers took part in a game that ended in a shutout, the official scorer must note that fact.

The Winning and Losing Pitchers

Overview: A winning and losing pitcher will be named for each game. In some cases the official scorer must make a judgment call to determine which pitchers qualify.

Determining the winning and losing pitchers

By the end of each game a winning and a losing pitcher will be selected. The following rules guide the official scorer in determining which pitcher within a team qualifies for each title.

The starting pitcher will receive credit for winning the game if:

• he pitches five complete innings or more, and

• his team is in the lead when he is substituted, and

• his team retains the lead for the remainder of the game.

Note: The "five innings" requirement pertains to games that lasted at least six innings. (A game may be terminated before the normal nine innings are complete when, for instance, the umpire-in-chief needs to end play because of bad weather.) If the game was terminated after only five innings, the pitcher must have pitched at least four complete innings to qualify to be winning pitcher (the other requirements listed above will still apply).

When the starting pitcher doesn't qualify to be the winning pitcher

If the starting pitcher doesn't meet the requirements, or if there is more than one substitute pitcher in the game, then:

1. If, while the starting pitcher is pitching, his team takes the lead and retains that lead throughout the game, the official scorer will award the winning pitcher title to the substitute pitcher he believes was the most effective.

2. If the score becomes tied, the selection of winning and losing pitchers starts anew.

3. If the opposing team takes the lead, no pitchers prior to that point will qualify for the title of winning pitcher. However, if the pitcher who was pitching when the opposing team took the lead continues to pitch in the game, retakes the lead, and his team retains that lead for the remainder of the game, he will be declared the winning pitcher.

4. A substitute pitcher will be declared the winning pitcher if he is the pitcher at the time his team takes the lead and his team retains the lead for the remainder of the game.

Exception: If that pitcher is ineffective in his role as pitcher, a new substitute begins pitching, and the new substitute pitcher is instrumental in helping his team retain the lead throughout the game, the new substitute pitcher will be credited with winning the game.

Note: Even when a substitute batter or substitute runner stands in for a pitcher, that pitcher is still considered the current pitcher. Runs scored by his team will still be credited to his turn as pitcher, and if his team takes the lead, he will receive the credit.

Losing pitcher

The losing pitcher will be the pitcher who leaves the game when the opposing team is ahead in the score, or if after he leaves, the opposing team pulls ahead in the score due to runners charged to him — provided that his team does not later tie the game or pull ahead.

Note: Runs will be charged to a pitcher if the scoring runners were on base at the time the pitcher was replaced.

Saves for Relief Pitchers

The official scorer can credit a substitute pitcher (a relief pitcher) with a "save." To qualify, all three of the following conditions must be met:

1. His team won and he was the last pitcher for his team, and

2. he is not named as the winning pitcher, and

3. one of these three conditions apply:

- the official scorer believes he pitched "effectively" for three or more innings, or

- his team was ahead by one, two or three runs when he entered the game, and he pitched at least one inning, or

- when he entered the game, the opposing team's potential tying runner was already on a base, at bat or on deck (scheduled to be the next batter up).

Note: On the last condition, since the "tying run" may be the batter on deck, this means up to five runs could possibly score to tie the game. The pitcher's team could have been ahead by four or five runs when he entered the game if he came into the game with two runners on base or with bases loaded.

The Winning Pitcher in the All-Star Game

In a non-championship game, for example, the All-Star Game, pitchers may be scheduled to take the mound for a predetermined number of innings. Typically the winning pitcher will be the pitcher in place when his team takes the lead and they retain the lead throughout the remainder of the game. The official scorer may credit the win to a subsequent pitcher however, if he believes the new pitcher is more deserving of the win.

Base Hits

Overview: A base hit is scored when the batter safely reaches first base — even if he is put out after that. There are exceptions.

Base hits *will* be scored when:

1. The batter successfully reaches first base or any other base when he hits a fair ball that lands on the ground or hits a fence before being touched by a fielder, or hits a ball over the fence in fair territory.

2. A batter successfully reaches first base or any other base after hitting a ball on which the fielders cannot make a play. The base hit will be scored even if the fielder misjudges the play or if one fielder interferes with another fielder in an attempt to make a play.

3. A batter reaches first base, or any other base, on a hit that takes an unexpected bounce, hitting a rock for example, and is unable to be caught in time by a fielder. The ball may also take a wild bounce after hitting the pitcher's rubber, home plate, or one of the other bases.

4. The batter hits a ball that rolls or flies into the outfield before being touched by a fielder, allowing the batter to reach first base or any other base.

Note: It will not be a base hit, however, if the scorer believes the fielder could have fielded the ball with "ordinary effort."

5. When the batter hits a fair ball that touches a runner or an umpire before being touched by a fielder.

Note: If an infield fly touches a runner who is not touching his base, both the batter and the runner will be called out. No base hit.

6. When on a hit a fielder tries without error to put out a runner in front of the batter, (fielder's choice), fails to put out that runner, and the official scorer believes the batter would have been safe at first if the fielder had tried to put him out instead.

Note: The official scorer is instructed to **favor the batter**, scoring a base hit when the batter reaches a base and "exceptionally good fielding" does not result in a putout.

A base hit will *not* be scored when

Even if a batter successfully reaches a base, he may not be credited with a base hit. In some cases, this is because a runner in front of him was forced out. Here are the reasons a batter may reach first base but will *not* be credited with a base hit.

1. A hit forces a runner out — or, if not for an error, the runner would have been forced out.

2. A batter safely reaches first, but a runner who is forced to advance fails to touch the next base to which he advances, and is called out on appeal by the defense. The scorer will attribute an at-bat to the batter, but not a base hit.

3. The pitcher, catcher, or infielders (without the aid of outfielders) put out a runner in front of the batter as that runner is trying to advance or trying to return to a base. The base hit will also not be scored if the fielders could have put out a runner, but made a fielding error.

4. Fielder's choice applies to a play in which a fielder, in the official scorer's judgment, could put out the batter at first base but attempts instead to put out another runner and fails. No base hit.

Note: The fielder must actually make an attempt to throw out the other runner, not simply turn his head towards that runner or fake a throw in that direction.

5. An umpire calls interference on a runner ahead of the batter, declaring that runner out.

Exception: The scorer will credit a base hit to the batter in this situation if he feels that the batter would have reached first base even if the interference had not occurred.

Base Hits	# Singles, Doubles, Triples, and Home Runs

The rule for singles, doubles, triples, and home runs is simple. On a hit, the official scorer credits a batter with a one-base hit if the batter reaches first base, a two-base hit if he reaches second, a three-base hit if he reaches third and a home run if he reaches home.

Base Hits	# If a Runner Ahead of the Batter is Put Out

Doubles: If the batter reaches second base, he is credited with only a one-base hit, not a two-base hit, if the runner ahead of him is put out at third (or if the runner would have been put out at third if it weren't for a fielding error).

Triples: If the batter reaches third base, he is credited with only a two-base hit, not a three-base hit, if the runner ahead of him is put out at home plate (or if the runner would have been put out at home if it weren't for a fielding error).

Note: Except for these two cases, the number of bases credited to a batter does not depend on the number of bases reached by the runner ahead of him.

Example: **Batter hits a double**

1. With no runners on base the batter hits a ball to left field that gets past the outfielder.

2. The batter safely reaches second base. **He will be credited with a two-base hit.**

Example: **Batter hits a double, but the runner ahead is put out.**

1. With a runner on first the batter hits a ground ball into the outfield.

2. The runner who was on first reaches third base safely, but only because an outfielder made a bad throw to third base. The batter reaches second.

3. Even though the batter reached second, in this situation **he will only be credited with a one base hit**.

| # Counting Base Hits

Running beyond a base, then being tagged out, counts.

If a batter touches a base, continues running beyond it to the next base, and is then tagged out, he will be credited for the last base he touched.

Example: The batter hits a ground ball into the outfield. He successfully reaches first base, continues his run to second but is put out. He will be credited with a one-base hit. If he was put out after running beyond second base he would be credited with a two-base hit, or if he was put out after running beyond third base, he would be credited with a three-base hit.

Awarded bases count as base hits.

If a batter is awarded two bases, three bases, or a home run, that number of bases will count as base hits. This will also be the case when the umpire awards bases for a fielder obstructing the batter on his way to first or obstructing a runner on whom a play is being made.

Fielder's choice doesn't count.

Fielder's choice takes place when a fielder opts to put out a runner ahead of the batter rather than the batter. When a batter gets a hit with one or more runners already on base, and he successfully reaches second base or beyond on the hit, the official scorer makes a judgment. He decides if the batter's hit qualifies as a two-base hit, a three-base hit, or if the batter only advanced to these bases because the fielder decided not to stop the batter or put him out.

Oversliding a base doesn't count as reaching a base.

If a batter overslides a base and is tagged out, he will *not* be credited with safely reaching that base.

Example: if a batter reaches first base, continues running towards second, slides into second but his slide takes him past the base and he is tagged out, he will only receive credit for a one-base hit.

Missing a base doesn't count as reaching a base.

If a batter hits the ball but while running misses touching a base, and is called out, he will only be credited with having reached the last base he actually touched.

Example: If a batter gets a hit that allows him to run to third, but misses second base in the process, and is called out on appeal by the defense, he will be credited only with a one-base hit. If he missed touching first base, he will not be credited with a hit at all, only an at-bat.

If a batter's hit wins the game

If the batter gets a game-winning hit he will receive credit for the number of bases advanced by the runner who scored the winning run at home. However, to receive this credit, the batter himself must safely have reached at least as many bases as were advanced by the winning runner.

Example: With a tie score of 5 to 5 in the last half of the last inning, with runners on second and third bases, a batter hits a ball into the outfield that bounces over the head of the right fielder. The runner from third base scores, winning the game. The runner from second base also reaches home plate. The batter is credited with a one-base hit, because that is the number of bases that the winning runner advanced to win the game. The batter, however, must fulfill his duties by running at least to first base to be credited with one-base hit. His team will win by a score of 6 to 5, even though two runners reached home.

If a home run wins the game

If the batter hits a home run out of the ballpark to win the game, the batter and all runners who were on base at the time will score. The home run will be counted.

Example: Base hits and home runs. With a tie score of 5 to 5 in the last half of the last inning, with runners on second and third bases, a batter hits the ball over the outfield wall for a home run. The two runners and the batter will score. The batter will receive credit for the home run — four-base hits. The final score of the game will be 8 to 5.

Runs Batted In (RBI)

Overview: Runs batted in is a measure of a batter's performance, crediting the batter with every run that scores as a result of his time at bat.

Runs-batted-in (RBI)

An RBI will be credited to the batter for every run scored as the result of that batter's:

- hit (in which he safely reaches a base).

- sacrifice fly.

- sacrifice out.

- hit that results in an out made in the infield, or an out by a "fielder's choice" (where a fielder opted to throw out a runner ahead of the batter).

- award of a base, that forces another runner to score because the bases were loaded (there were runners on first, second, and third bases). The awarded bases may be due to:

  - being walked (i.e., the batter received a base-on-balls).

  - a pitch touching the batter.

  - a call of interference or obstruction.

RBI and home runs

A home run will result in one RBI for the batter himself and one RBI for every runner on base when the home run was hit. A home run with bases loaded, for example, will result in four RBI's.

RBI and errors

An RBI will be credited to the batter if, with zero or one out:

- a runner from third scores, and

- and error is made on the play, and

- the runner from third would have scored even without the error.

An RBI will *not* be credited for runs scored when:

- a batter hits a ground ball resulting in a force double play or a force reverse double play.

- a fielder makes an error on a play at first base that otherwise would have resulted in a force double play.

The scorer determines if an RBI counts when fielders make errors.

The scorer must determine if an RBI should be credited when a fielder hesitates or makes an error — for instance, if a fielder holds onto the ball, or does not throw to the correct base.

The official rules instruct the scorer to:

Credit the RBI if the runner runs continuously, without pausing.

Do not credit the RBI if the runner pauses, then runs after noticing the fielder's hesitation or mistake.

In the second case, the run will be attributed to fielder's choice, not to the batter.

Note: Force Double Plays and Reverse Force Double Plays

A **force double play** is a play in which two runners are forced to run and are put out. A **reverse force double play** is a play in which the possibility of a force out exists for two runners, but the trailing runner is put out first, removing the force on the runner ahead of him. This requires the defense to tag the runner ahead of him for the second out, not just tag the base.

Sacrifices

Sacrifices will be scored when:

A sacrifice occurs when a batter hits or bunts the ball in a way that is likely to put him out, for the purpose of advancing another runner. This is a strategic move by the offensive team. As a result, batters are not penalized with an at-bat that results in an out.

Sacrifice flies

The official scorer will record a sacrifice fly when these conditions are met:

- there is zero or one out,
- a fly ball or a line drive is hit into the outfield,
- any fielder catches the fly ball or line drive in the outfield to put the batter out,
- a runner already on base scores a run on the play.

Note: If the fielder misses the catch, and a runner scores, the sacrifice fly will still be recorded as long as the official scorer believes the runner would have scored even if the catch was made. In this case, the sacrifice fly will be scored even if another runner is forced out by the batter's hit.

Sacrifice bunts

The official scorer will record a sacrifice bunt when:

- With zero or one out, the batter bunts, putting him out at first base, but advancing at least one other runner.

  A sacrifice bunt will also be recorded if the batter is safe at first because of a fielding error, but would have been put out had the error not occurred.

- With zero or one out, the batter bunts, and the fielders, in an errorless play, try but do not succeed in putting out a runner in front of the batter. The batter may be safe on first.

Exception: If after the bunt:

- the fielders try but fail to put out a runner in front of the batter, and
- in the official scorer's judgment, had the fielders instead attempted to put out the batter at first, and without error, the batter would still have been safe at first,

then the batter will be credited with a base hit, not a sacrifice.

A sacrifice bunt will *not* be scored when:

- any runner is put out trying to advance on the bunt. The batter will instead be charged with an at-bat.

- in the official scorer's judgment, the batter is bunting to reach a base, not to sacrifice himself for the purpose of advancing a runner.

  Note: In making this judgment, when the batter's motive may be questionable, the scorer is instructed to allow the batter the "benefit of the doubt" and record a sacrifice bunt.

Sacrifice flies and bunts

A sacrifice fly differs from a sacrifice bunt in that a runner must score on a sacrifice fly, but a runner only needs to advance on a sacrifice bunt.

Stolen Bases

A stolen base is defined as a successful advance by a runner that is not enabled by:

- a hit
- a putout
- a fielder's error
- a force out
- fielder's choice (a fielder's decision not to throw the runner out as he is stealing the base, even though he could have).
- a catch that was missed
- a wild pitch
- a balk

If the runner steals a base and the pitcher pitches wild or the catcher throws wild

The following rules are in place for these situations:

- If the run to steal a base begins before the pitcher throws his pitch, and the pitch results in a wild pitch or the catcher misses the catch, the runner will still be credited with a stolen base.

- If the runner is able to advance beyond that stolen base as a result of the wild pitch or the missed catch, the scorer will record the wild pitch or the missed catch in addition the stolen base.

- if the runner steals a base and the catcher makes a wild throw in his attempt to put out the runner, the runner will be credited with a stolen base.

- If the runner is able to advance beyond that stolen base as a result of the catcher's wild throw, or any other runner is able to advance as a result of the wild throw, the scorer will record an error for the catcher in addition to the stolen base.

Stolen bases and run-down plays

The following applies if a runner begins to steal a base, or takes a lead off of a base, and becomes caught in the run-down play (where fielders on either side of him attempt to put him out). If the runner is not put out and manages to advance to the next base (not the result of a fielder's error), he will be credited with a stolen base. If another runner takes this opportunity to also steal a base both runners will be credited with stolen bases. If one runner steals a base but the other safely returns to his original base, the runner who advances will be credited with the stolen base.

| **Stolen Bases** | Caught Stealing | continued |

A runner will be charged with "caught stealing" when:

If in attempting to steal a base a runner is put out, or if in the official scorer's opinion he would have been put out except for a fielder's error, the runner will be charged with "caught stealing." This will be the case when the runner:

- attempts to steal a base and is tagged out.

- overslides a base during a steal and is tagged out.

- is thrown out when he takes a lead off of a base and is "picked off" (tagged for an out before he can return to the base).

A runner will *not* be charged with "caught stealing" when:

- he attempts to steal when the catcher misses a pitch, but is put out.

- he is obstructed and a base is awarded.

| **Stolen Bases** | Situations in which Runners Will Not Receive Credit for a Stolen Base |

Runners will *not* be credited with a stolen base:

1. If two (or three) runners attempt to steal a base at the same time and any one of them is put out before reaching the base, none of the runners will be credited with a stolen base.

2. If a runner in the act of stealing a base overslides the base, either when advancing to the base or returning to the base, and is tagged out, he will not be credited with a stolen base.

3. When a runner stealing a base is only safe because a fielder missed or mishandled a throw:

- the runner will not receive credit for a stolen base, but instead will be charged with "caught stealing" — even though he is safe on the base.

- an assist will be credited to the fielder who made the throw.

- an error will be charged to the fielder who missed or mishandled the throw.

4. If in stealing a base a runner reaches it only because the fielder opted to allow the steal and not to make the play, the runner will not be credited with a stolen base. The scorer will record the advance as "fielder's choice."

Putouts and Assists

Overview: Putouts and assists are measures of a fielder's performance.

A fielder will receive credit for a putout when:

- he catches a hit ball before it touches the ground, either on fair or foul territory.

- he catches a thrown ball to put out a batter or a runner running to a base.

- he tags a runner who is not touching his base.

Putouts and Assists | Automatic Putouts

The catcher will receive credit for an automatic putout when:

- the batter is out on the call of an illegally batted ball (a ball is illegally batted, for example, when the batter hits the ball with one or both of his feet outside of the batter's box).

- the batter bunts a ball on the third strike, and the ball goes foul.

- **Exception:** If the bunt is a fly ball into foul territory, and it is caught before hitting the ground, the fielder who caught the fly ball will be credited with the putout.

- the batter is out because he was touched by the ball he just hit.

- the batter is called out because he interfered with the catcher.

- the batter is called out for missing his turn at bat.

- a batter refuses to advance to first base after being walked (after receiving a base-on-balls).

- a runner is called out for refusing to advance from third base to home to win the game.

Other types of automatic putouts

Other automatic putout situations occur when:

- an infield fly is not caught and the batter is called out. Credit for the putout goes to the fielder who, in the judgment of the official scorer, would have caught the fly.

- a runner is called out because he was touched by a ball hit into fair territory, infield flies included. The putout will be credited to the fielder closest to the ball when it touched the runner.

- a runner is called out because he ran more than three feet away from the baseline to avoid being tagged. The fielder who was trying to tag him will receive credit for the putout.

- a runner is called out because he passed a runner in front of him. The fielder who was closest to the runner as he passed the other runner will receive credit for the putout.

- a runner is called out because he runs the bases in reverse order (to try to confuse the other team). The fielder who was covering the base from which he began his reverse run will receive credit for the putout.

continued on next page

| Putouts and Assists | Automatic Putouts | continued |

- the batter is out on the call of an illegally batted ball (a ball is illegally batted, for example, when the batter hits the ball with one or both of his feet outside of the batter's box).

- the batter bunts a ball, on the third strike, that goes foul.

  Exception: if the bunt sends the ball on a fly into foul territory and it is caught before hitting the ground, the fielder who caught the fly ball will be credited with the putout.

- the batter is out because he was touched by the ball he just hit

- the batter is called out because he interfered with the catcher.

| Putouts and Assists | Assists |

Credits for assists

An assist is a credit given to each fielder who assisted the fielder who received credit for the putout. An assist is awarded if he fields a batted or a thrown ball, throwing or deflecting it toward another fielder whose play results in an out. An assist will be awarded even if the other fielder mishandles the ball and fails to put out the runner. If the play in question is a run-down play, only one fielder will be credited with the assist.

Even though a fielder can receive credit for an assist if he deflects the ball, it only counts if the deflection has an effect — for instance, if the ball's trajectory was affected, or the ball's movement was slowed, enabling another fielder to make the out.

An assist *will* be credited when:

- a fielder throws or deflects a thrown or batted ball, and that action leads to an out.

- a fielder throws or deflects a thrown or batted ball, and that action leads a runner to be called out for interference or called out for running outside of the base path.

- a pitcher who, if a catcher misses a catch on a third strike, fields the ball and throws it to another fielder for an out. (This could occur, for instance, if the catcher misses the catch and the pitcher is able to get to the ball before the catcher.)

Credits for putouts and assists on double plays and triple plays

In plays in which two or three runners (including the batter-runner) are put out, credits for assists or putouts go to every fielder who took part (unless a misplay also took place, as

discussed above). The play must take place between the time the pitch is made and the time that the ball is either 1) dead, or 2) the pitcher, in his pitching position, takes possession of the ball.

Note: If one of the putouts was the result of an appeal by the defense, even if the appeal is granted after the pitcher has taken possession of the ball, the credits for the assists and the putout will be counted.

An assist *will not* be credited when:

- the pitcher simply strikes out the batter.

- after catching a pitch, the catcher makes a play that puts out a runner — for instance, if the catcher tags a runner coming into home, or makes a throw to put out a runner attempting to steal a base.

- a fielder throws wild — even if, in spite of the wild throw, a runner is eventually thrown out on the play.

Fielding Errors

Overview: An error is charged whenever a fielder makes a misplay — mishandling of the ball that either extends a runner's time on a base, allows a runner to advance, or extends a batter's time at bat. An error may be charged regardless of whether a batter or runner advances on the play.

Exception: An error must entail a "physical" mishandling of the ball. If a fielder simply handles the ball slowly, but is in control of the ball, an error will not be charged. Similarly, if a fielder misjudges a play, an error will not apply.

Fielding Errors	Seven Ways an Error Can be Charged

An error will be charged when:

1. a fielder mishandles the ball, extending a runner's stay on bases, allowing a runner's advance, or extending a batter's time at bat.

2. a fielder fields a batted or thrown ball at first base but fails to tag the batter or the base (if in the scorer's judgment he could have put him out).

3. similarly, a fielder fields a batted or thrown ball in a force play but fails to tag the runner or the base (if in the scorer's judgment he could have put him out).

4. a fielder makes a wild throw, missing an opportunity to put out a runner or the batter-runner.

Exception: A wild throw made during an attempt to put out a runner stealing a base will not be counted as an error.

5. a fielder makes a wild throw during an attempt to put out a runner, and that throw enables that runner, or another runner, to advance.

Note 1: Although this may seem unfair, an error will also be charged against a fielder if runners are able to advance because his throw hit the ground and bounced unpredictably, or bounced off the pitcher's rubber or a base, or touched an umpire or a runner — even if the throw itself was accurate. The official scorer must account for every advance made by the offense, and advances in these situations will be attributed to a fielder's error.

Note 2: On any wild throw, regardless of how many runners advanced or how many bases they reached, only one error will be charged.

6. a fielder fails to catch or stop an accurately thrown ball, and a runner advances. If this occurs on a throw to second base the official scorer will decide if that throw should have been fielded by the second baseman or by the shortstop. If the official scorer believes the fielder who made the throw threw it without good reason, then the fielder who made the throw will be charged with the error.

7. a fielder is charged with obstruction, or with defensive interference, causing the umpire to award one or more bases. An error will be charged against the fielder.

Note: Similar to the wild throw situation, only one error will be charged on a call of obstruction or defensive interference, regardless of how many runners advanced or how many bases they attained as a result. An error will *not* be charged if, in the official scorer's opinion, the infraction did not have an effect on the outcome of the play.

| # Assists and Fielding Errors

Additional plays made after a fielder's misplay will be treated like a new play.

If a fielder makes a mistake (making an error or otherwise mishandling the ball) the subsequent action will be treated as if it were a new play.

Meaning, a fielder who handled the ball before or during the misplay will not receive credit for an assist (assuming a runner was eventually put out on the play). That is, unless that fielder handles the ball again after the misplay occurred.

If a ball goes through a fielder's legs

A fielder does not need to touch the ball to be charged with an error. Balls that "could have been" handled by a fielder, but weren't, will be considered errors. For instance, if a ball goes between a fielder's legs, or a pop fly is completely missed, the official scorer will charge that fielder with an error — as long as he believes that the fielder, with "ordinary effort," could have caught the ball.

| # Errors Will Not be Charged

An error will *not* be charged when:

1. the catcher, after catching a pitch, throws to a base to catch a runner stealing, and his throw goes wild.

2. a fielder's wild throw is not to blame — meaning, if the official scorer believes the runner or runners would have reached their bases safely even if the throw was accurate, then no error will be charged.

3. a fielder makes a wild throw in an effort to complete a double- or triple-play.

Note 1: In the three situations above, when as a result of the wild throw a runner advances to a base beyond the base he was attempting to reach, or if the wild throw enables any other runners advance, an error *will* be charged.

Note 2: If the fielder on the receiving end of a throw mishandles the catch, allowing a runner or runners to safely reach a base, then that fielder will be charged with an error. The fielder who threw the ball, assuming he threw it accurately, will be credited with an assist, as if the receiving fielder's error had not occurred.

4. a fielder mishandles the ball — a fly ball, line drive, ground ball, or a throw by another fielder — but the batter-runner or any runner who is forced to advance is put out at that base in spite of the misplay.

5. with zero or one out and a runner on third base, a fielder intentionally allows a fly foul ball to hit the ground, rather than catch it for an out.

Note: This instance describes a strategic decision for which the fielder should not be penalized with an error. If he had caught the ball, it would remain in play and the runner from third may be likely to score at home. By letting it drop, the ball is dead and runners stay put.

An error against a pitcher or a catcher will *not* be charged in certain cases.

The pitcher and catcher handle the ball much more frequently than the other fielders. Special rules are in place regarding acts that will not be considered errors. An error against a pitcher or a catcher will **not** be charged when:

1. a pitcher:

- pitches four balls, or
- hits the batter with a pitch, or
- throws a wild pitch, or
- pitches but his pitch is missed by the catcher.

Even though the batter may be awarded or otherwise advance to first base as a result, errors are not charged.

2. the catcher misses a catch.

3. a runner or runners advance because of a wild pitch, a balk or a missed catch.

4. a wild pitch results in a fourth ball, but because it goes wild:

- it allows the batter to advance to second base or beyond.
- it allows a runner or runners who are forced to advance to reach a base beyond their forced base.
- it allows any other runner, not forced, to advance one or more bases.

5. a wild pitch on the third strike enables the batter to reach first base. Although no error will be charged, both a strikeout and a wild pitch with be recorded for the pitcher.

6. the catcher misses a pitch on the third strike, enabling the batter to reach first base. Although no error will be charged, a strikeout and a passed ball with be charged against the pitcher and the catcher, respectively.

7. on a wild pitch or a missed catch that occurs on the third strike, the catcher is still able to make a play, putting the batter out by tagging him or by throwing to first, but other runners advance. The official scorer will record:

- a strikeout for the pitcher.
- the putout to the catcher, or the putout to the first baseman and an assist to the catcher.
- the base advances of the runners.

Consecutive Streaks

Guidelines for cumulative performance records

There are three types of consecutive records that concern the official scorer:

Consecutive hitting streaks

A batter's consecutive hitting streak refers to the number of consecutive times he came to bat and made a hit that put him safely on base.

A hitting streak will continue if a batter's appearance at the plate results in a base-on-balls, he is hit by a pitch, the umpire calls interference, or he hits a sacrifice bunt. His streak will end if he hits a sacrifice fly.

Consecutive-game hitting streaks

A batter's consecutive-game hitting streak refers to the number of consecutive games in which, at some point in the game, he made a hit that put him safely on base.

Consecutive playing streaks

A player's consecutive playing streak refers to the number of consecutive games he played.

His streak will continue if:

- the player plays at least one half-inning on defense, or

- an at-bat results in his reaching a base or being put out, or

- he is ejected from the game, even if he is ejected before he can fulfill the requirements above.

If the player simply pinch-runs for another player, this appearance is not enough to extend his streak.

Note: Cumulative performance records and suspended games

In calculating consecutive streaks, a player's performance in a suspended game that needs to be rescheduled and resumed on another day will be treated as if the game were completed on the day it was originally scheduled.

Reporting the Scoring Results

Decisions must be made within twenty-four hours of the game's conclusion

The official scorer's decisions for the game must be reported within twenty-four hours of the game's conclusion, Although some decisions are made immediately, the official scorer is required to finalize all of the game's decisions within twenty-four hours. After that point, changes to any of the judgment decisions in his report can only made with approval of the league president. The scorer will also need to submit a reason for the change, or the erroneous entry.

Note: Games must reach "regulation game" status before they can become official and be counted in the official record. In general, this means that at least half the game must have been completed (see page 190 for details about when a game becomes a regulation game).

Reporting | # Results

Called, forfeited, and suspended games

The reporting times will also apply to called, forfeited, and suspended games. In the case of suspended games — where a game had to be rescheduled due to weather or other reasons — the official scorer must submit his report up to thirty-six hours after that game has been resumed and completed.

Reconstructing suspended and protested games

Suspended games must be resumed using the same playing situation as when the game was suspended. This means the game will pick up using the same batting order, fielders, pitcher, etc., as if a time delay had not occurred. The same is true if a protest is upheld (a rare event where an umpire's decision

is found to be in error, and it affects the game's outcome). A protested game, when rescheduled, will pick up from the exact play that caused the protest. Runners, if any, will be placed in the same position and the same batter will come to bat with the same count of balls and strikes. The official scorer's information will serve as the official record on which to base reconstruction of the game.

Consistency

The official scorer's responsibilities are spelled out in the official rule book to ensure consistency in record keeping from game to game. If any situations arise that are not covered in the rule book, the official scorer has the authority to impose rules (just like an umpire can impose decisions for situations not covered in the rules).

The official scorer and the umpire

The official scorer:

- does not have the authority to override an umpire's decision.

- must abide by the official rules of baseball.

- if he notices that a batter has come to bat out of turn, he must refrain from informing the umpire or the teams. (Similarly, if an umpire notices that a batter is batting out of turn, he also must refrain from reporting this fact. They must wait until one of the teams takes action.)

> **Note: Changing sides too soon**
>
> The official scorer will notify the umpire if the offense and the defense start to change sides before a third out is made.

Included in the scorer's report:

The official scorer's final report will include:

- the date the game was played
- where it was played
- the names of the two teams involved

- names of the umpires officiating at the game
- the score
- records of each player's performance during the game (as discussed in this chapter)

Individual Championships

Overview: Several awards are given to individual players for their performance over the course of the season. This section describes how they are selected.

The individual batting champion will be the player with the highest batting average or slugging percentage. However, during the season he must have come to bat at least this number of times:

$$\text{the number of games scheduled for each team in his league} \times 3.1$$

Example: If a team is scheduled to play 162 regular games in a regular season (not including play-off games) then the batter chosen for the individual batting champion must have come to the plate at least 502 times.

The number of times he came to the plate is the total of the number of:

- his official at-bats
- base-on-balls that were pitched to him
- times he was hit by a pitch
- sacrifice bunts
- sacrifice flies
- times he was awarded first base on a call of interference or obstruction

Note: If a batter did not meet the requirement for minimum number of appearances at the plate — for instance, if he only came to bat 499 times rather than 502 times — one additional calculation can be tried. If the minimum required number of appearances, 502, is used in place of 499 when calculating his batting average, and his batting average is still the highest, he will be awarded the title of batting champion.

See page 226 for information on the batting average.

The individual pitching champion will be the pitcher with the lowest ERA (earned run average). As a minimum requirement he must have pitched a number of innings equal to the number of regular games scheduled in that season. The rules in the Major Leagues differ from the Minor League — the Minor League's minimum requirement is lower. See page 228 for information on ERAs.

Major Leagues:

$$\text{minimum number of innings} = \text{number of scheduled games in the regular season}$$

With 162 games scheduled in a season, a pitcher must have pitched at least 162 innings to qualify.

Minor League:

$$\text{minimum number of innings} \times 80\% = \text{number of scheduled games in the regular season}$$

If 144 games are scheduled in a season, a Minor League pitcher must have pitched at least 115 innings to qualify.

Individual Championships | Fielding Championships

The individual fielding champion will be the player with the highest fielding average. If the player's position is:

- **catcher**, he must have played in at least one-half of the games scheduled for each team during the season.

- **infielder or outfielder**, he must have played in at least two-thirds of the games scheduled for each team during the season.

- **pitcher**, he must have pitched at least as many innings as the number of games scheduled for each team during the season.

Exception: If a pitcher does not meet the minimum requirements for pitching champion, but in his fielding role:

- he has a fielding average that is equal or higher than other fielders, and

- he had more opportunities to field the ball during the season (even though he played in a fewer number of innings),

that pitcher will be selected to be the fielding champion.

The Official Statistician

Another position appointed by each league president is the official statistician. For every player and every game the statistician will create tables displaying all individual and team records. The rules state that, in his report, the statistician must:

- identify each player by his first and last name,

- indicate whether each player bats right-handed, left-handed, or switches between the two,

- for each fielder, indicate if he throws with his right or left hand.

Only players who actually played in the position listed in the batting order are included. If, for instance, a starting player bats in the first inning but is replaced before he becomes a fielder, he will not be credited for that fielding position. However, all players listed in the game's starting lineup will receive credit for being in the game. Games scheduled at the end of the season to break a tie within a division will also be included in the official statistician's records.

Calculations

Calculated statistics include:

- Batting average (AVG)

- Slugging percentage (SLG)

- On-base percentage (OBP)

- Pitcher's earned run average (ERA)

- Percentage of games won (W-L)

- Fielding percentage (FP)

Statistics

Overview: The following pages explain the meaning, and show the math, for some common baseball measures of performance.

Statistics | Batting

Statistics: Batting

Batting performance can be described by three different statistics:

- Batting Average (AVG)
- Slugging Percentage (SLG)
- On-Base Percentage (OBP)

Batting average (AVG):

Batting average measures a player's batting performance. It is calculated by dividing the number of times he got a base hit by the total number of times at bat.

$$\text{Batting average} = \text{AVG} = \frac{\text{Number of base hits}}{\text{Number of times at bat}}$$

For example, if a player has been at bat 200 times and has had 66 base hits, his batting average would be:

$$\text{Batting average} = \frac{66 \text{ base hits}}{200 \text{ times at bat}} = .330$$

A higher AVG indicates better batting performance.

Slugging Percentage (SLG):

Slugging percentage, unlike batting average, takes into account the number of bases the batter reached with each base hit — if it was a single, double, triple, or home run.

$$\text{Slugging percentage} = \text{SLG} = \frac{\text{Number of bases reached}}{\text{Number of times at bat}}$$

A single = 1 base, a double = 2 bases, a triple = 3 bases, and a home run = 4 bases. Let's say a player has been at bat 200 times and had 66 base hits. Those hits consisted of 50 singles, 10 doubles, 2 triples and 4 home runs. He therefore reached a total of 92 bases.

$$
\begin{array}{rcl}
50 \text{ singles x } 1 & = & 50 \text{ bases} \\
10 \text{ doubles x } 2 & = & 20 \text{ bases} \\
2 \text{ triples x } 3 & = & 6 \text{ bases} \\
4 \text{ home runs x } 4 & = & 16 \text{ bases} \\
\hline
66 \text{ hits} & = & 92 \text{ total bases reached}
\end{array}
$$

His slugging percentage is .460:

$$\text{Slugging percentage} = \frac{92 \text{ bases reached}}{200 \text{ times at bat}} = .460 \text{ bases per at-bat}$$

On-base percentage (OBP)

The on-base percentage indicates the ability of the batter to get on base. This includes base hits, walks, and getting to first by being hit by the pitch.

This total number of times a batter got on base is divided by the sum of:

- the number of times at bat,
- the number of walks,
- the number of times he got to first by being hit by the pitch, and
- the number of sacrifice flies.

$$OBP = \frac{\text{Hits} + \text{Walks} + \text{Hit by the Pitch}}{\text{At Bats} + \text{Walks} + \text{Hit by the Pitch} + \text{Sacrifice Flies}}$$

For example, if after 508 times at home plate, a player got 152 hits, was walked 59 times, and was hit by a pitch 9 times:

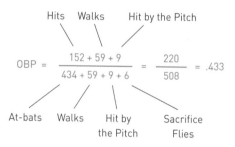

His OBP equals .433. A higher number indicates better batting performance.

Statistics | # Pitching

Pitching performance can be measured by:

- Earned run average (ERA)
- Win-loss percentage (W-L)

Earned run average (ERA)

The earned run average measures pitching performance. The number represents the average number of runs a pitcher gives up in nine innings. An earned run is any run scored off of a specific pitcher. Runs scored as the result of an error do not count as earned runs because they are not considered to be the pitcher's fault. The other team must "earn" the run for it to be counted in the ERA.

ERA is calculated by:

$$ERA = \frac{\text{number of runs earned by the other team}}{\text{number of innings pitched}} \times 9$$

For example, if a pitcher gives up 18 earned runs in his first 60 innings:

runs earned by
the other team

innings

$$ERA = \frac{18}{60} \times 9 = 2.70 \text{ runs per inning}$$

innings he pitched

Less is more!

The ERA measures how many runs the pitcher is likely to give up in nine innings. Fewer is better — a lower number indicates better pitching performance.

W-L percentage (win-loss percentage) for a pitcher

This is a simple calculation measuring a pitcher's past performance. It simply takes the number of games he won and divides it by the total games he pitched.

$$W\text{-}L \text{ percentage} = \frac{\text{games won by a pitcher}}{\text{total games pitched}}$$

If a pitcher has pitched 19 games, winning 12 of them and losing 7, his W-L percentage would be:

$$W\text{-}L \text{ percentage} = \frac{12 \text{ games won}}{19 \text{ total games played}} = .632 \text{ wins per game}$$

Or put another way, he wins 63.2% of the time.

| Statistics | Fielding |

A fielder's performance is measured by his fielding percentage (also referred to as "fielding average").

Fielding percentage

The fielding percentage is determined by dividing a fielder's successful fielding attempts by his total number of fielding attempts. This is a measure of his "chances" of successfully fielding the ball in future plays.

Fielding percentage is calculated by:

$$\text{Fielding percentage} = \frac{\text{putouts + assists}}{\text{putouts + assists + errors}} = \text{percentage of success}$$

For example, if a fielder has 198 putouts and 214 assists, but made 5 errors, his fielding percentage would be:

$$\text{Fielding percentage} = \frac{198 \text{ putouts} + 214 \text{ assists}}{198 \text{ putouts} + 214 \text{ assists} + 5 \text{ errors}}$$

$$= \frac{412 \text{ successful attempts}}{417 \text{ total attempts}} = .988$$

| Statistics | Team Standings |

Towards the end of the season, in addition to knowing which team is ahead in the standings, it is helpful to know just how many games are needed to win the title.

Magic number

The magic number in baseball indicates the minimum number of future games a team needs to win in order to secure the season title.

The number is calculated by adding 1 to the number of games remaining to be played, then subtracting the number of games by which that team is ahead:

$$\text{Magic number} = \frac{\text{number of}}{\text{games remaining}} + 1 - \frac{\text{number of games}}{\text{ahead of the}}_{\text{second place team}}$$

For example, the first place team has 90 wins, putting them 3 games ahead of the second place team, which has 87 wins. The first place team has 14 games remaining in the season. To calculate their magic number:

$$\text{Magic number} = 14 \text{ games remaining} + 1 - 3 \text{ games ahead} = 12 \text{ games}$$

Note: At some point into the season, the magic number calculation will also indicate when it is no longer possible for a team to make it into the playoffs.

W-L percentage (win-loss percentage) for a team

A win-loss percentage for a team is similar to the win-loss percentage for a pitcher:

$$\text{W-L percentage} = \frac{\text{games won by a team}}{\text{games they played}}$$

Glossary

Appeal is a claim by a player or manager, to the umpire, that a rule has been broken.

Assist is an award attributed to a fielder who fields or contacts the ball, intentionally or unintentionally, prior to a putout being recorded.

At-bat describes a player's turn in the batter's box.

Automatic out is an out attributed to a violation of the rules.

Awarded base is a base "given" to a batter or runner, allowing him to advance to the base without risk of being put out.

Balk is a penalty charged against the pitcher, when a runner or runners are on base, typically for attempting to deceive a runner. A balk results in an award of one base to all runners.

Ball is a pitch that does not pass within the strike zone.

Base coaches are members of a team's coaching staff positioned near first base and third base to advise the batter and runners.

Base line is a direct line between the bases.

Base-on-balls (walks) is an award of first base given to the batter after the pitcher has pitched four balls (four pitches outside the strike zone).

Base path is a 6-foot wide lane, three feet to either side of the base line.

Batter's box is an area to either side of home plate, where the batter stands while at bat.

Batter-runner is the name used for a batter who has just finished his turn at bat and has become a runner.

Batting order, also called the lineup, refers to the sequence in which players will come to bat.

Called game (terminated game) is a game that has been prematurely ended by the umpire.

Catcher interference also known as defensive interference, occurs when a catcher interferes with the batter.

Championship Season (Regular Season) is the period during which the teams play their 162 scheduled games, prior to the playoffs.

Coach is a team member assigned specific responsibilities to help improve the team's performance.

Dead ball is a ball no longer in play because the action on the field is temporarily suspended.

Defense is the team that is pitching and fielding.

Defensive interference occurs when any fielder (typically the catcher) interferes with the batter.

Designated hitter (DH) is a player named to bat for the pitcher.

Double-header refers to two games played on the same day.

Earned Run Average (ERA) is the average number of runs a pitcher gives up in 9 innings.

Earned Runs are runs made by the opposing team for which the pitcher is responsible.

Ejection occurs when, as penalty for a serious violation, the umpire sends a team member to the clubhouse, banning him from further play.

Errors are fielding mistakes that benefit the offense.

Fair ball is a ball hit within the foul lines.

Fair territory is the area within the foul lines. The foul lines and the foul poles themselves are within fair territory.

Field umpires are the umpires positioned at the bases.

Fielder is any one of 9 players on the defensive team.

Fielder's choice describes a situation in which a fielder decides to make a play other than to put out a batter running to first base.

Fly ball is a ball hit by the batter that travels up into the air and has not yet touched the ground. Also see *ground ball* and *line drive*.

Force plays are plays in which a batter or runner is at risk of being put out because he is forced to advance when the batter becomes a runner.

Forfeit is a situation in which the umpire-in-chief declares one team the winner, with an automatic score of 9-0, as penalty for a serious rule violation.

Foul ball is a ball hit outside the foul lines, or that lands in fair territory but crosses the foul line before passing first or third base.

Foul territory is the area outside of the foul lines, and outside the foul poles.

Foul tip is a ball that is barely hit by a batter's swing and travels directly into the catcher's mitt.

Grand slam home run is a home run made with a runner on every base.

Ground ball is a hit ball that bounces or rolls along the ground. Also see *fly ball* and *line drive*.

Ground rule double is an award of two bases for a hit that bounces or is deflected out of play.

Ground rules are special rules that cover situations unique to a specific ballpark. Each ballpark has its own ground rules.

Illegal pitch is a pitch that violates some aspect of the rules.

Infielder is a fielder playing one of four fielding positions — first, second, third base or shortstop.

Infield fly is a ball hit high into the infield that can be easily caught by a fielder.

Infield Fly Rule is a call by the umpire, made while an infield fly is still in the air, that automatically puts out the batter.

Inning is a segment of the game in which each team has a chance to bat. Typically, games are 9 innings long.

Interference is an act that illegally hinders a play. Types of interference include:
• Offensive interference
• Defensive interference
• Umpire interference
• Spectator interference

Judgment call is a call made by an umpire in which his decision is final

League is a group of baseball teams. Major League Baseball consists of the American League and the National League.

Line drive is a ball hit sharply by a batter that travels horizontal to the ground. Also see *ground ball* and *fly ball*.

Manager is the person designated by a club to direct the team and to communicate with the umpires.

MLB Major League Baseball is the organization that controls professional baseball in the United States and Canada.

Obstruction occurs when a fielder unfairly blocks or otherwise impedes a runner's advance.

Offense is the team at bat.

Offensive interference occurs when a member of the offense interferes with a live ball or a fielder making a play.

Official scorer in an official appointed by Major League Baseball to record the events of a game.

Official statistician is a person appointed by the league president to keep the statistical records of a game.

Out occurs when a batter or runner is disqualified from advancing the bases. Three outs ends a team's turn at bat for that inning.

Outfielder is a fielder playing one of three positions in the outfield.

Pitcher's mound is an eighteen-foot diameter area in the infield, on which the pitcher stands.

Pitcher's rubber (plate) is a 6" x 24" rectangle on the pitcher's mound. The pitcher must touch it with his foot when pitching.

Pivot foot is the pitcher's foot that is in contact with the pitcher's rubber. It is the right foot for right-handed pitchers, the left foot for left-handed pitchers.

Plate umpire is another name for the umpire-in-chief, since he is positioned at home plate. Among other things, the plate umpire calls pitches as balls or strikes.

Protest describes a team's appeal to a league president to overrule an umpire's call that was not in keeping with the rules, and that affected the game. If upheld the game will be replayed from the point of the play in question.

Putout is an act by a fielder that causes a runner or a batter-runner to be out.

Rain check is a ticket issued to a spectator for entry to a rescheduled game.

RBI see *Runs Batted In.*

Regular Season see Championship Season.

Regulation game describes a game that has progressed far enough to become official and be entered into the record books. A game becomes a regulation game when the losing team has completed batting 5 half-innings.

Removal refers to the ejection of a player from the game.

Retouch refers to a runner retreating to a base to touch it again.

Reverse force double play refers to play in which the batter hits the ball, forcing one or more runners to advance, and the fielders throw out the batter first (removing the force) before tagging out a runner ahead of him.

Rubber see *Pitcher's rubber.*

Run down occurs when a runner is caught between bases by two fielders who throw the ball between them to try to put out the runner.

Runs Batted In (RBI) is a measure of batting performance, referring to the number of runs that scored due to a batter's performance.

Sacrifice bunt occurs when, with 0 or 1 out, a batter bunts, putting himself out but allowing one or more runners to advance. The bunt will not be scored as a sacrifice bunt if any runners are put out on the play.

Sacrifice fly occurs when, with 0 or 1 out, a batter hits a fly ball or a line drive that is caught for an out, but which allows one or more runners to score — even if other runners are put out on the play.

Set position is one of two pitching positions. (*Windup* is the other.)

Shutout is a game in which one team does not score any runs.

Spectator interference occurs when a spectator enters or reaches into the field, affecting a play.

Squeeze play describes a play in which a batter bunts in an attempt to allow a runner on third base to score.

Stolen base is an advance on a base that is not due to a hit or awarded base.

Strike occurs when a batter swings at a pitch and misses, or fails to swing at a pitch that passes through the strike zone.

Strike zone is an area above home plate, defined by the width of home plate and the size of the batter. The strike zone defines whether a pitch will be called a ball or a strike.

Suspended game is a game in which play is stopped (due to poor weather, for instance) but will be resumed either later that day or on another day.

Tag occurs when a fielder, securely holding the ball, touches a base with any part of his body, or touches a runner with either the ball or with his glove holding the ball.

Tag up is the act of a runner touching his original base, or returning to touch his original base. When a fielder catches a fly ball. a runner must tag up before advancing.

Terminated game (called game) is a game prematurely ended by the umpire.

Umpire is an official appointed by Major League Baseball to officiate at a game.

Umpire interference occurs when a hit ball touches an umpire, or the umpire gets in the way of a catcher or his throw.

Umpire-in-chief is the head umpire. He is typically positioned at home plate, and is also referred to as the plate umpire.

Walk see *base-on-balls.*

Wild pitch is a pitch thrown too high, low or wide to be caught by the catcher.

Wild throw is a throw that is too high, low or wide to be caught by a fielder.

Windup position is one of two pitching positions. (*Set* is the other.)

Index

The Authors

Dan Formosa, Ph.D.

Dan Formosa is a consultant in design and design research, and has developed innovative products for companies worldwide. Dan spent his grammar school years in Hoboken, NJ, the site of baseball's first recorded game. He went on to earn degrees in design, ergonomics and biomechanics. He started his career as a member of the design team for IBM's first personal computer. Other work ranges from the design of medical products to day-to-day consumer items. His work is included in the permanent collection of the Museum of Modern Art. He was a founding member of Smart Design, and has received design awards worldwide.

Dan lectures frequently about design and information around the world. He spends much of his time working in New York City, across the river but still within sight of Hoboken's old Elysian Fields.

Paul Hamburger

Paul Hamburger is a communications designer in New York City with broad experience in graphics, information design and product branding. Before opening his own firm, Paul was Director of Graphic Design at Smart Design. In addition, he has been an adjunct professor teaching graphic design at Parsons School of Design in New York City since 1997. His work has won numerous awards and he has been recognized in books and magazines.

Growing up in the streets of Brooklyn, Paul was an accomplished player of stoopball. As a Mets fan, Paul is bitter and resentful toward the overwhelming success of other local baseball organizations. He lives in the past, nostalgic for the glory that was the mid eighties.